MathFlare

Name: _______________________

Class: __________

Teacher: _______________________

Introduction

As parents and educators, we recognize the pivotal role mathematics plays in shaping a child's academic journey and future success. Yet, the path to mathematical proficiency can often seem daunting, fraught with challenges and complexities. That's where the transformative power of MathFlare Workbooks shine through, illuminating the way forward with clarity, precision, and purpose.

Introducing MathFlare Workbooks – a beacon of guidance, a testament to excellence, and a catalyst for achievement. Crafted with meticulous care and expertise, MathFlare Workbooks stand as paragons of educational excellence, designed to nurture young minds, ignite a passion for learning, and develop a deep-rooted understanding of mathematical concepts.

Picture this: your child eagerly delves into the pages of Mathflare Workbook, greeted by a step-by-step guide illuminated with vivid examples that demystify complex mathematical concepts. With each turn of the page, they embark on a journey of discovery, encountering thoughtfully curated practice questions that reinforce learning and hone problem-solving skills. And when they unveil the answers to those very questions, a sense of accomplishment blossoms within them – a tangible reward for their hard work and dedication.

But MathFlare Workbooks are more than just tools for learning; they are pathways to comprehension, fostering a deep-seated understanding of mathematical concepts through a sequential, logical flow. From fundamental principles to advanced problem-solving strategies, every chapter builds upon the last, ensuring a robust foundation upon which future knowledge can be constructed.

As parents, we yearn for nothing more than to see our children thrive, to witness the spark of inspiration ignited within them as they conquer academic challenges with confidence and poise. MathFlare Workbooks serve as partners in this noble endeavor, offering not just practice questions, but the keys to unlocking a world of opportunity.

And for teachers, MathFlare Workbooks stand as invaluable allies in the quest to cultivate mathematical proficiency in the classroom. With answers readily available, instructors can focus on guiding and nurturing their students, confident in the knowledge that MathFlare Workbooks provide a solid framework upon which to build.

In the pages of MathFlare Workbooks, we find not just the promise of academic excellence, but the seeds of a brighter tomorrow. So let us embrace the power of mathematics, let us champion the journey of learning, and let us pave the way for a generation of young minds poised to shape the world. With MathFlare Workbooks as our guide, the possibilities are infinite, and the future, bright.

Table of Contents

MathFlare
Grade 2
MATH WORKBOOK
Step by Step Guide and Essential Practice with Answers
Addition Subtraction
Multiplication
Place Value and Expanded Notations
Geometry
MathFlare Publishing

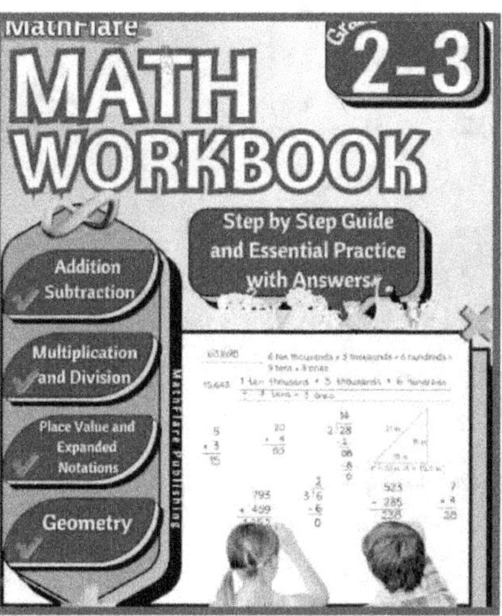
MathFlare
Grade 2-3
MATH WORKBOOK
Step by Step Guide and Essential Practice with Answers
Addition Subtraction
Multiplication and Division
Place Value and Expanded Notations
Geometry
MathFlare Publishing

MathFlare
Grade 3
MATH WORKBOOK
Step by Step Guide and Essential Practice with Answers
Multiplication and Division
Decimals
Place Value and Expanded Notations
Fractions and Geometry
MathFlare Publishing

MathFlare
Grade 1
MATH WORKBOOK
Step by Step Guide and Essential Practice with Answers
Counting and Numbers
Addition and Subtraction
Place Value and Expanded Notations
Understanding Time
MathFlare Publishing

MathFlare
Grade 1-2
MATH WORKBOOK
Step by Step Guide and Essential Practice with Answers
Counting and Numbers
Addition and Subtraction
Place Value and Expanded Notations
Understanding Time
MathFlare Publishing

MathFlare
Grade 3-4
MATH WORKBOOK
Step by Step Guide and Essential Practice with Answers
Addition Subtraction
Multiplication Division
Place Value and Expanded Notations
Fractions and Geometry
MathFlare Publishing

MathFlare
Grade 4
MATH WORKBOOK
Step by Step Guide and Essential Practice with Answers
Addition Subtraction
Multiplication Division
Place Value and Expanded Notations
Fractions and Geometry
MathFlare Publishing

MathFlare
Grade 4-5
MATH WORKBOOK
Step by Step Guide and Essential Practice with Answers
Multiplication Division
Place Value and Expanded Notations
Fractions and Geometry
Unit Conversion
MathFlare Publishing

MathFlare
Grade 5
MATH WORKBOOK
Step by Step Guide and Essential Practice with Answers
Multiplication Division
Place Value and Expanded Notations
Fractions and Geometry
Unit Conversion
MathFlare Publishing

MathFlare
Grade 5-6
MATH WORKBOOK
Step by Step Guide and Essential Practice with Answers
Multiplication Division
Place Value and Expanded Notations
Fractions and Geometry
Units and Statistics
MathFlare Publishing

MathFlare
Grade 6
MATH WORKBOOK
Step by Step Guide and Essential Practice with Answers
Integers and Statistics
Arithmetic and Pre-Algebra
Fractions and Geometry
Ratio and Percentage
MathFlare Publishing

MathFlare
Grade 6-7
MATH WORKBOOK
Step by Step Guide and Essential Practice with Answers
Arithmetic and Pre-Algebra
Ratio, Percent Proportion
Geometry
Statistics
MathFlare Publishing

MathFlare
Grade 7
MATH WORKBOOK
Step by Step Guide and Essential Practice with Answers
Pre-Algebra
Ratio, Percent Proportion
Geometry
Statistics
MathFlare Publishing

MathFlare
Grade 7-8
MATH WORKBOOK
Step by Step Guide and Essential Practice with Answers
Pre-Algebra
Ratio, Percent Proportion
Geometry and Cartesian Plane
Statistics
MathFlare Publishing

MathFlare
Grade 8-9
MATH WORKBOOK
Step by Step Guide and Essential Practice with Answers
Pre-Algebra
Ratio, Proportion and Percentage
Linear Equations
Geometry and Cartesian Plane
MathFlare Publishing

MathFlare
Grade 8
MATH WORKBOOK
Step by Step Guide and Essential Practice with Answers
Pre-Algebra
Percentage
Linear Equations
Geometry
MathFlare Publishing

Rational Numbers: Operations

Positive and negative integers are whole numbers that can represent quantities greater than zero and less than zero, respectively.

Positive Integers: Positive integers are whole numbers greater than zero. They are denoted by the numbers 1,2,3,4...

Negative Integers: Negative integers are whole numbers less than zero. They are denoted by placing a negative sign ("-") before the numbers, such as $-1, -2, -3, -4,...$

The positive integers are used to represent the number of objects, scores, etc. whereas the negative integers can be used to represent debt, losses, temperatures below freezing points, etc.

Let's solve some problems:

1. $6 - (-8) - 9$

- Start by simplifying within the parentheses:

$$-(-8) \text{ becomes } 8.$$

- Rewrite the expression with the simplified part:

$$6 + 8 - 9.$$

- Now perform addition and subtraction from left to right:

$$6 + 8 = 14, \text{ then } 14 - 9 = 5$$

2. $(-5) - (-3) + 10$

$$(-5) + 3 + 10$$

$$(-5) + 3 = -2, \text{ then } -2 + 10 = 8$$

Order of Operations (PEMDAS)

The order of operations, often remembered by the acronym PEMDAS, stands for:

- **Parentheses**: Perform operations inside parentheses first.
- **Exponents**: Evaluate exponents (powers and roots) next.
- **Multiplication and Division**: Perform multiplication and division from left to right.
- **Addition and Subtraction**: Perform addition and subtraction from left to right.

The order of operations helps to clarify which operations should be performed first in a mathematical expression to ensure consistent and accurate results.

- **Parentheses**: Evaluate expressions within parentheses first. If there are nested parentheses, start with the innermost ones and work your way out.

    1. Example: $2 \times (3 + 4) = 2 \times 7 = 14$

- **Exponents**: Evaluate expressions with exponents (powers and roots) next.

    1. Example: $2^3 + 4 = 8 + 4 = 12$

- **Multiplication and Division**: Perform multiplication and division from left to right.

    1. Example: $2 \times 3 + 4 = 6 + 4 = 10$

    2. Example: $6 \div 2 \times 3 = 3 \times 3 = 9$

- **Addition and Subtraction**: Perform addition and subtraction from left to right.

    1. Example: $2 + 3 \times 4 = 2 + 12 = 14$

    2. Example: $10 - 4 \div 2 = 10 - 2 = 8$

Equations and Expressions

Solving One-Step Equations

Solving one-step equations involves finding the value of the variable that makes the equation true. In a one-step equation, there is only one operation (addition, subtraction, multiplication, or division) performed on the variable.

The goal is to isolate the variable on one side of the equation by performing inverse operations.

For example:

Given the equation $6 = -3z$, where we want to solve for z.

The given equation is already in the form of a one-step equation, with z being multiplied by -3.

To isolate z, we need to perform the inverse operation of multiplication, which is division.

Divide both sides by -3:

$$\frac{6}{-3} = \frac{-3z}{-3}$$

Simplify:

$$-2 = z$$

So, the solution to the equation is $z = -2$.

When we substitute the value of z = −2 back into the original equation, 6 = −3(−2), it simplifies to 6 = 6. This confirms that our solution is correct because it satisfies the original equation.

Solving Two-Step Equations

Solving two-step equations involves finding the value of the variable that makes the equation true. In a two-step equation, two operations (addition, subtraction, multiplication, or division) are performed on the variable.

The goal is to isolate the variable on one side of the equation by performing inverse operations in the reverse order of operations.

For example:

Given the equation 18 = (10 + b) − 2, where we want to solve for b.

To solve for b, we need to undo the operations that have been performed on b.

1. Undo the subtraction by adding 2 to both sides:

$$18 + 2 = (10 + b) - 2 + 2$$

$$20 = 10 + b$$

2. Undo the addition by subtracting 10 from both sides:

$$20 - 10 = 10 + b - 10$$

$$10 = b$$

So, the solution to the equation is b = 10

Let's substitute b = 10 back into the original equation to verify if it satisfies the equation:

Original equation:

$$18 = (10 + b) - 2:$$

Substitute b = 10:

$$18 = (10 + 10) - 2$$

simplify:

$$18 = 20 - 2$$

$$18 = 18$$

Solving Equations (One Side)

Solving one-step equations involves performing a single operation to isolate the variable and find its value.

Let's solve an equation step by step: **16 + x = 31**

1. **Identify the Goal:**

    The goal is to isolate the variable x on one side of the equation.

2. **Simplify the Equation:** Combine like terms on both sides of the equation, if necessary.

    The equation is already simplified.

3. **Undo Addition or Subtraction:** If there's addition or subtraction involving the variable, undo it by performing the opposite operation on both sides of the equation.

Since x is being added to 16, we'll undo this operation by subtracting 16 from both sides of the equation:

$$16 + x - 16 = 31 - 16$$

4. **Isolate the Variable**: Ensure that the variable is alone on one side of the equation.

$$x = 15$$

5. **Check Your Solution**: Substitute the value of x back into the original equation to verify that it satisfies the equation.

$$16 + 15 = 31$$

$$31 = 31$$

The equation is balanced.

Evaluate Expressions

Evaluating expressions involves substituting given values for variables in an expression and then performing the indicated operations to find the result.

For example: Let's evaluate 4x – 10, when x = 3:

Step 1: Substitute the given value for the variable:

Replace every occurrence of x in the expression 4x – 10 with the given value, which is 3:

$$= 4(3) - 10$$

Step 2: Perform the operations:

Perform the indicated operations according to the order of operations (PEMDAS - Parentheses, Exponents, Multiplication and Division, Addition and Subtraction):

$$= 4 \times 3 - 10$$

Step 3: Simplify:

Calculate the result:

$$12 - 10 = 2$$

Rational Numbers: Operations
Evaluate Expressions.

1. $(-8) - 6 + (-5) =$

2. $(-2) - 5 - (-7) =$

3. $-(-1)(7) =$

4. $-(-4)(10) =$

5. $-7 \div 4 =$

6. $3 - 3 - (-4) =$

7. $(-5) - 10 + (-8) =$

8. $7 - 4 - (-3) =$

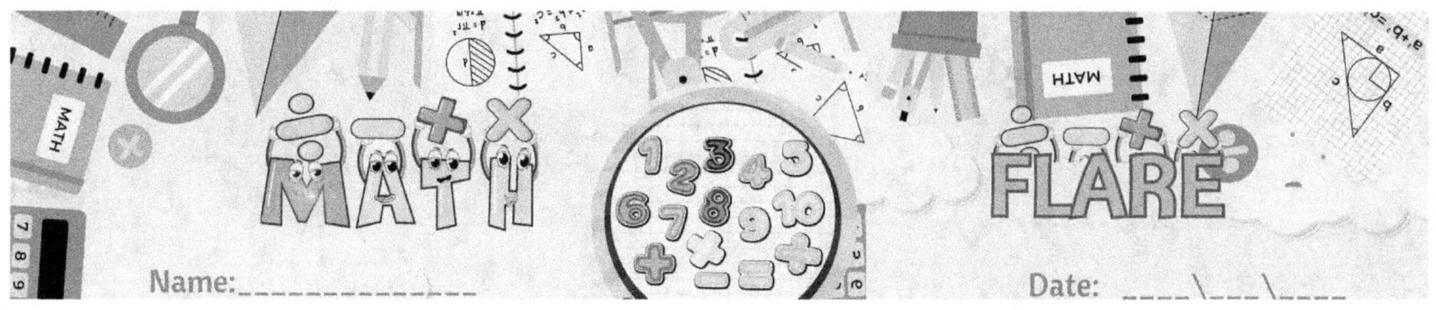

9. $6 - (-4) - (-9) =$

10. $2 + (-2) + (-6) =$

11. $2 \div -3 =$

12. $-9 \div -9 =$

13. $-4 \div -8 =$

14. $1 \div -8 =$

15. $(9)(8)(-7) =$

16. $(4)(-4)(-7) =$

17. $(6)(8) =$

18. $10 + 10 - (-8) =$

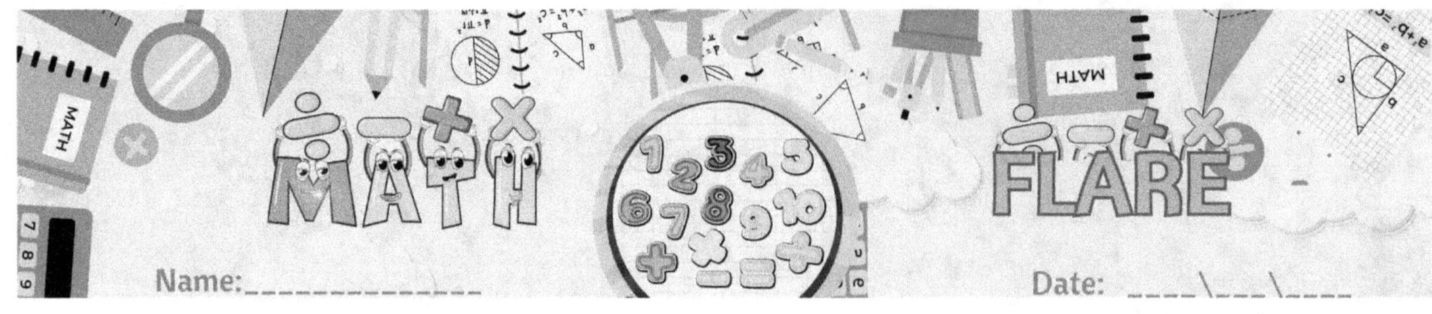

19. $(4)(-4)(1) =$

20. $(-9) - 7 - 6 =$

21. $5 + (-6) + (-3) =$

22. $(-2)(-3)(-7) =$

23. $-(-10)(3) =$

24. $-2 \div -9 =$

25. $-4 \div -6 =$

26. $1 \div -3 =$

27. $(-7) - 2 + (-5) =$

28. $(-5)(-7) =$

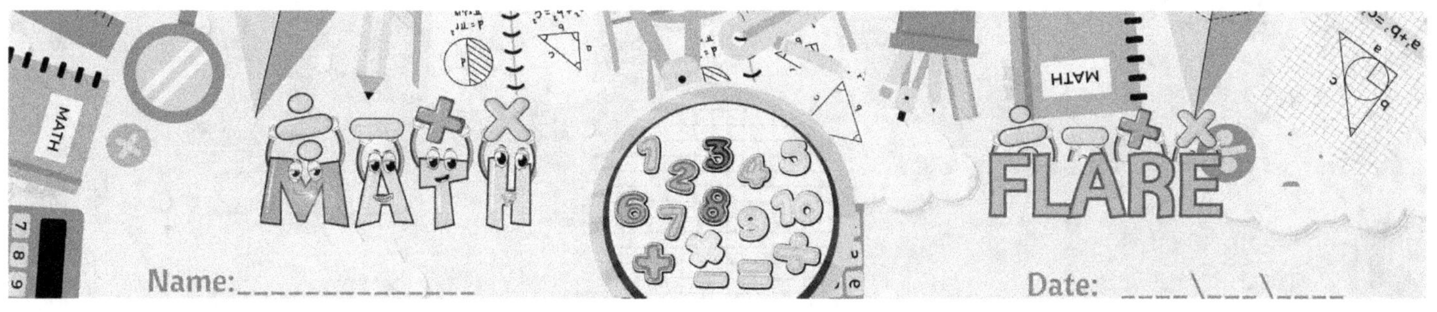

29. $-4 \div 5 =$

30. $3 + 7 - (-8) =$

31. $(-9)(4)(9) =$

32. $4 + (-8) + (-2) =$

33. $(2)(-4)(-2) =$

34. $(-4)(-10) =$

35. $(2)(-9)(-6) =$

36. $(7)(-2)(-7) =$

37. $(-2) - 3 + (-8) =$

38. $2 + (-2) - 9 =$

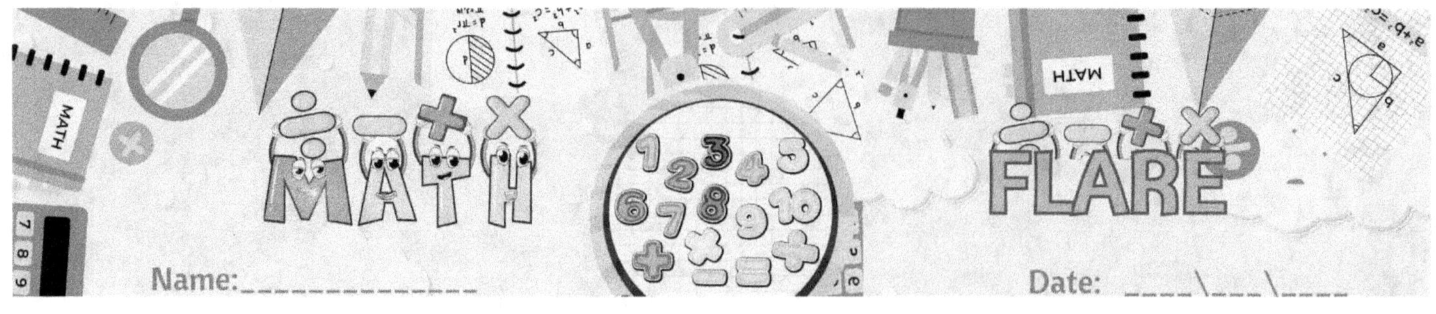

39. $7 + (-2) - (-3) =$

40. $9 + (-6) - 3 =$

41. $4 + 2 - (-2) =$

42. $(9)(-6) =$

43. $-3 \div 9 =$

44. $(-8) + 7 - 5 =$

45. $(-10)(-8)(1) =$

46. $4 + 8 - (-4) =$

47. $(-5) - 4 - 9 =$

48. $9 \div 6 =$

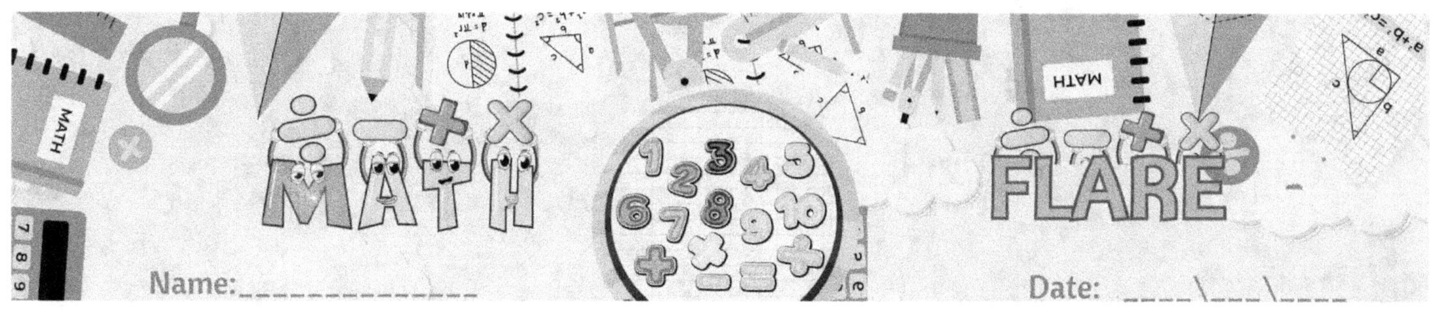

49. $(7)(3)(1) =$

50. $10 \div -6 =$

51. $8 + (-6) - 2 =$

52. $(3)(-6) =$

53. $-(-3)(-6)(-2) =$

54. $(-9)(-2)(-9) =$

55. $(3)(4) =$

56. $4 - 9 - (-5) =$

57. $(-1)(7) =$

58. $(3)(-10) =$

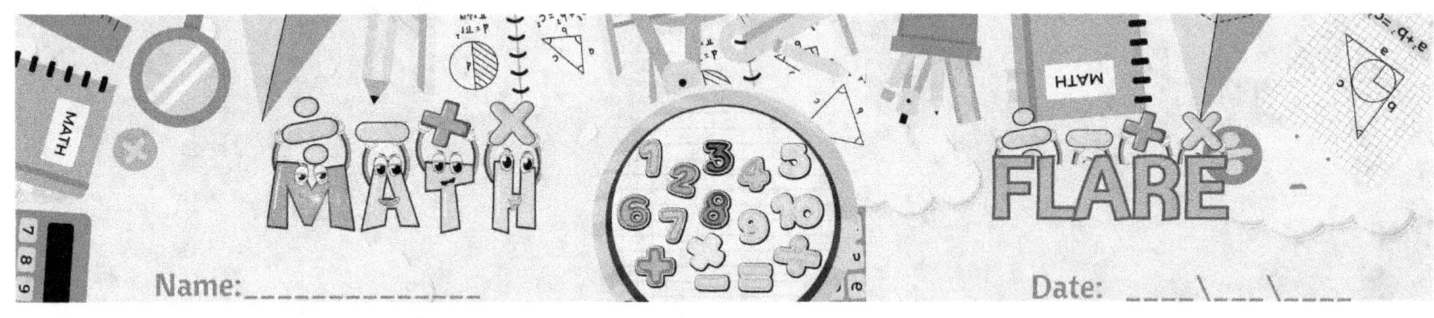

Order of Operations (PEMDAS)

1. $1 + 10^2 =$

2. $2 + 4 + 7 =$

3. $(4 + 4) \times (9 + 9) =$

4. $8(2 + 1) =$

5. $6 \times 5 =$

6. $(8 + 2)^2 + (7 + 5)^2 =$

7. $(10 \times 2) - (4 + 3) =$

8. $4 + 10 + 10 =$

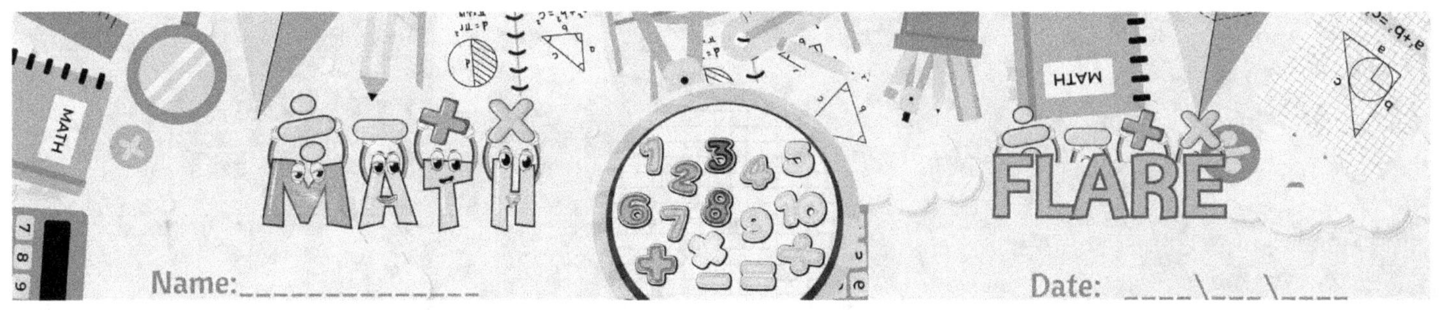

9. $(9^2) \times (10^2) + 1 =$

10. $1 \times 8 \times 8 =$

11. $2 + 3 + 1 =$

12. $(9^2) \times (7^2) + 6 =$

13. $7 + 6 + 9 + 3 =$

14. $2 + 6 + 9 + 2 =$

15. $4 + 6 + 5 =$

16. $2 + 7 + 2 =$

17. $1 + 3^2 + 8 + 2^2 =$

18. $(8^2) \times (7^2) + 2 =$

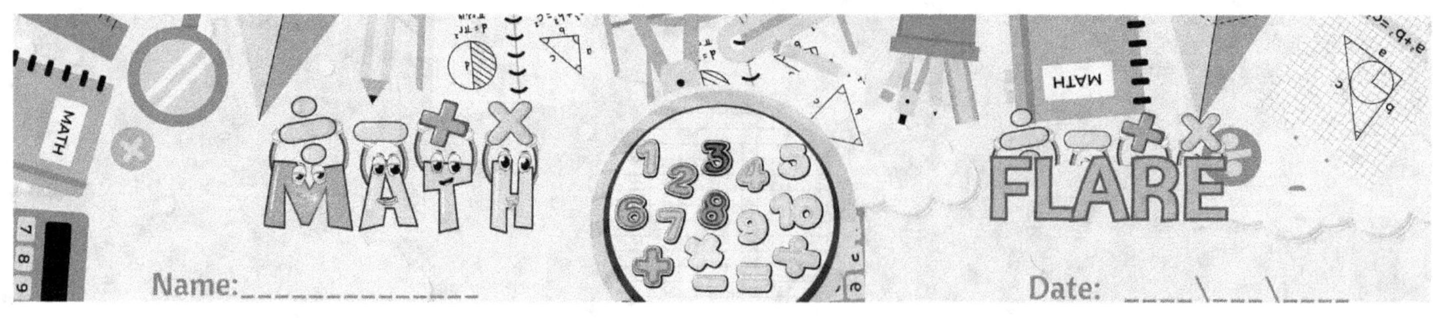

19. $(5^2) \times (8^2) + 5 =$

20. $3 + 9 + 2 =$

21. $10 \times 1 =$

22. $(8 + 6)^2 + (7 + 1)^2 =$

23. $(7^2) \times (1^2) + 10 =$

24. $(2^2) \times (10^2) + 2 =$

25. $(8 + 5) \times (9 + 6) =$

26. $3 \times (5 + 10) =$

27. $(5 + 6)(8 + 9) =$

28. $6 \times 10 \times 2 =$

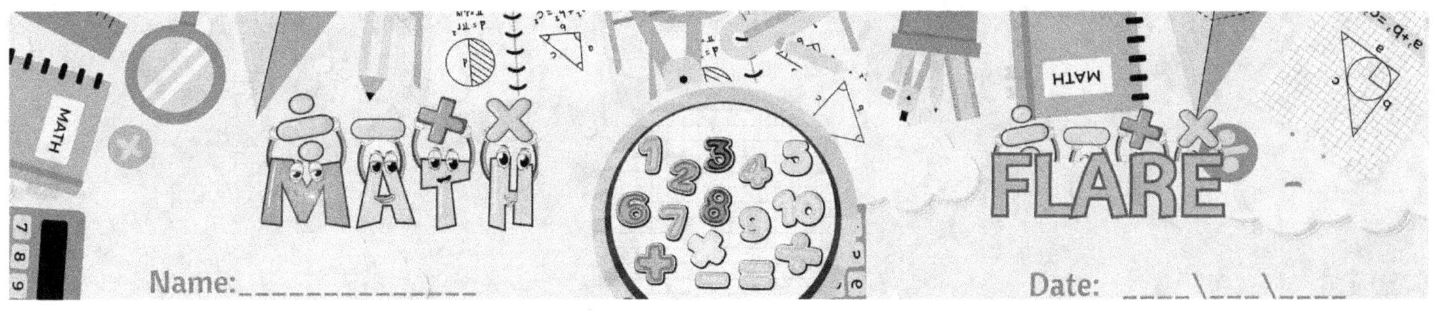

29. $(1 + 4)^2 + (3 + 9)^2 =$

30. $(5 \times 10) - (4 + 5) =$

31. $(9 + 1) \div 7 =$

32. $1 \times (9 + 1) =$

33. $1 + 2 + 2 =$

34. $1(9 + 1) =$

35. $(1^2) \times (2^2) + 3 =$

36. $(9^2) \times (5^2) + 10 =$

37. $(4 + 5)^2 =$

38. $6 + 3 + 3 =$

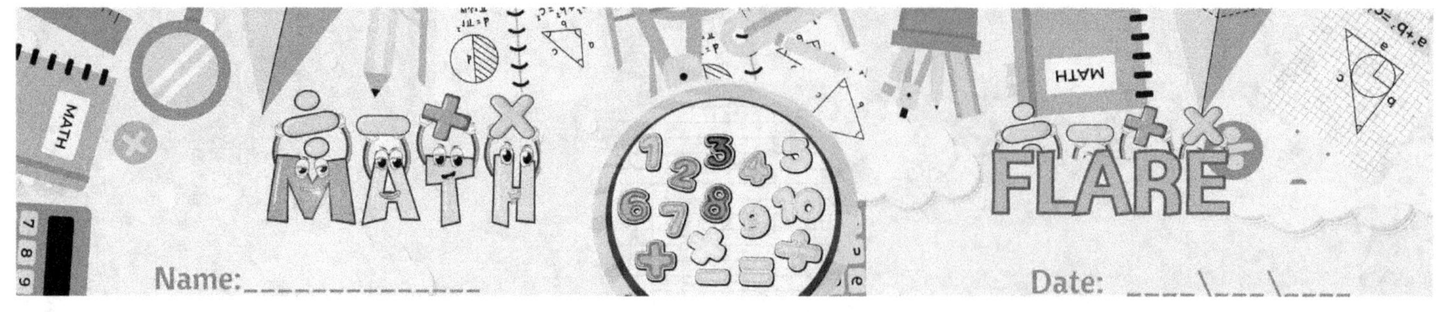

39. $(3 + 6) \times (6 + 10) =$

40. $8 + 10 + 9 =$

41. $3 + 6 + 9 =$

42. $10 + 3 + 7 + 9 =$

43. $(5 + 5) \times (6 + 8) =$

44. $(8 + 9)^2 =$

45. $1 \times 9 \times 2 =$

46. $4 \times 4 =$

47. $5 \times (7 + 10) =$

48. $9(6 + 9) =$

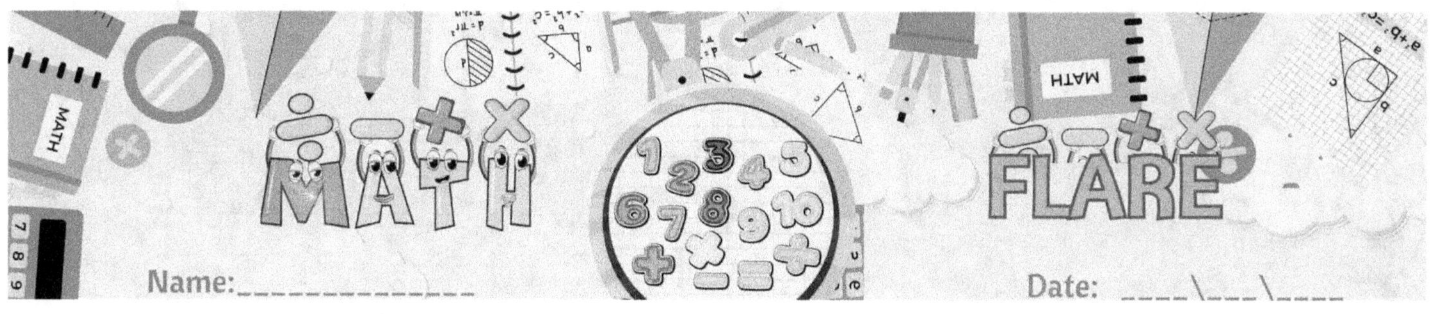

49. $5(5 + 3) =$

50. $(1 + 8) \div 3 =$

51. $10(4 + 9) =$

52. $3 \times 8 \times 7 =$

53. $(5 \times 10) - (3 + 4) =$

54. $5 \times 1 + 2 =$

55. $8 + 5^2 =$

56. $(6^2) \times (8^2) + 5 =$

57. $2 + 2 - 6 + 8 =$

58. $3 \times 3 =$

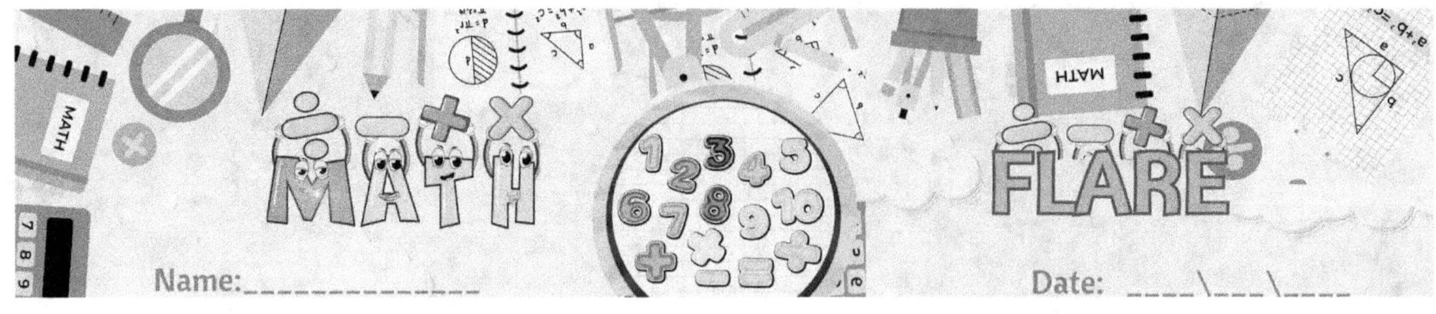

59. $(10 + 5)^2 =$

60. $1 + 1 - 6 + 8 =$

61. $(4^2) \times (8^2) + 7 =$

62. $3 + 6^2 + 5 + 9^2 =$

63. $(7 + 4) \div 3 =$

64. $(7 + 5) \div 2 =$

65. $(2 + 3) \div 10 =$

66. $(8^2) \times (9^2) + 4 =$

67. $10 \times 8 \times 8 =$

68. $10 + 7 + 8 + 3 =$

69. $1 \times (6 + 4) =$

70. $4 + 7 + 5 =$

71. $4 + 6^2 =$

72. $(10 + 7)^2 =$

73. $4 + 10^2 =$

74. $(2^2) \times (1^2) + 7 =$

75. $1 + 2 + 9 + 5 =$

76. $(1 + 7) \div 2 =$

77. $(1 + 1) \div 7 =$

78. $2 \times 7 + 7 =$

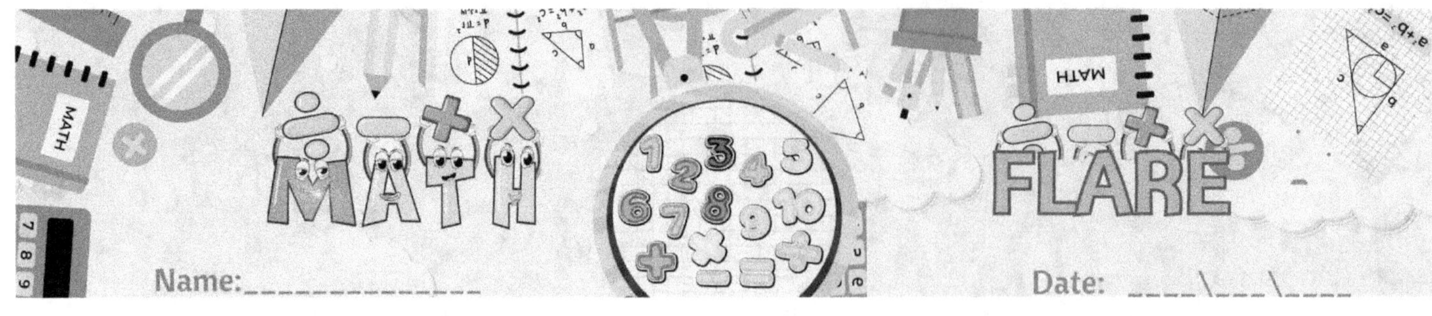

79. $10 + 7 + 9 + 10 =$

80. $(5^2) \times (4^2) + 4 =$

81. $3 + 4 + 10 =$

82. $(7 + 3)(1 + 6) =$

83. $3 \times 6 \times 6 =$

84. $9 \times (8 + 4) =$

85. $3 \times 8 =$

86. $7 + 1^2 + 3 + 7^2 =$

87. $(6^2) \times (10^2) + 6 =$

88. $(4^2) \times (7^2) + 5 =$

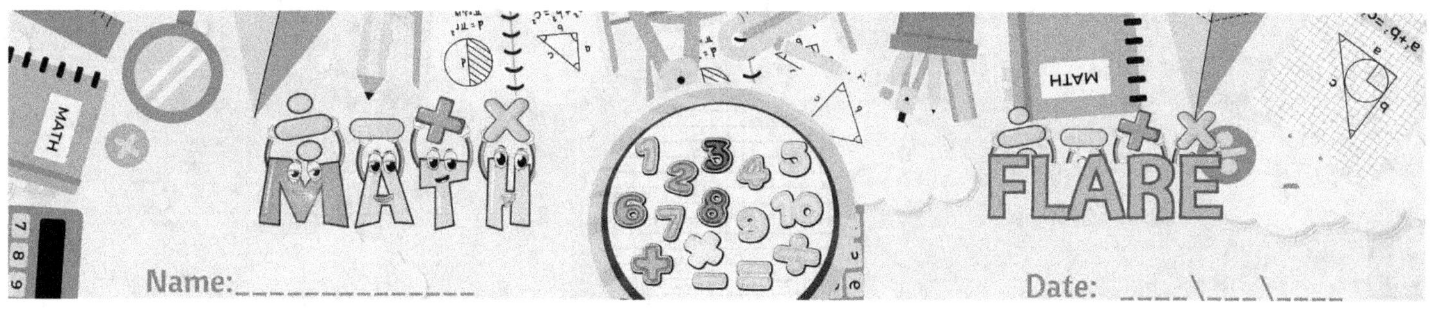

89. $(8 + 8) \div 7 =$

90. $4(9 + 4) =$

91. $5 + 8^2 + 7 + 4^2 =$

92. $7 + 2 + 3 =$

93. $(2 + 10) \div 1 =$

94. $9 + 6 - 5 + 9 =$

95. $5 \times 3 + 4 =$

96. $(2 + 10) \div 8 =$

97. $(8 + 8)^2 + (8 + 5)^2 =$

98. $(8 + 1)(4 + 2) =$

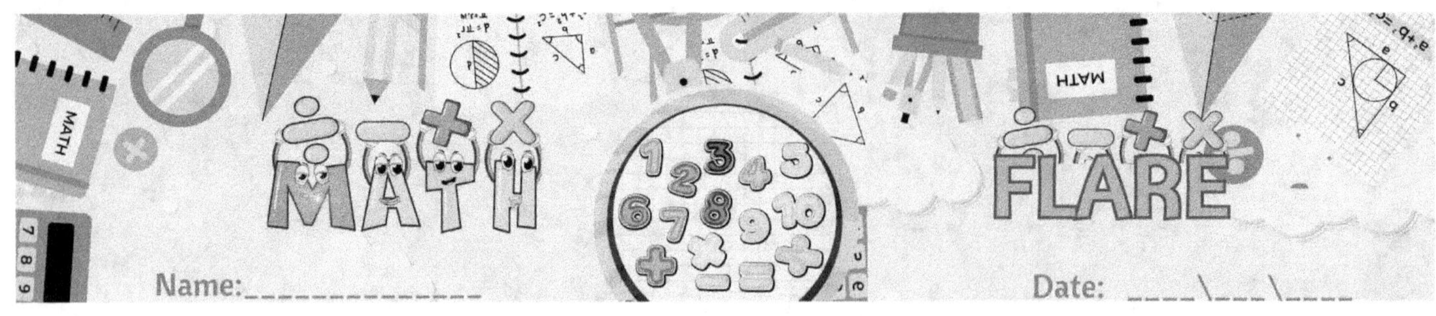

Solving One-Step Equations

Solve for the variable.

1. $y + 10 = 16$

2. $-3 + m = 4$

3. $-8a = -16$

4. $-4m = -8$

5. $-9 + z = -7$

6. $13 = x + 7$

7. $10m = 60$

8. $2 = s$

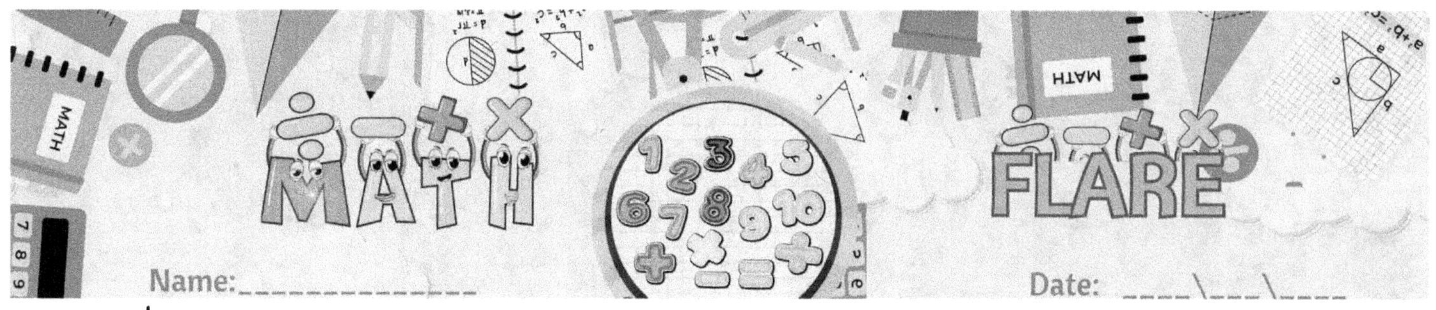

9. $\dfrac{b}{4} = 1$

10. $6 = x - 4$

11. $\dfrac{b}{1} = 9$

12. $11 = z + 3$

13. $-9 + a = 0$

14. $y - 9 = 0$

15. $y + 1 = 11$

16. $16 = b + 6$

17. $8s = 16$

18. $b - 6 = -5$

19. $15 = x + 10$

20. $z - 4 = 4$

21. $y - 5 = 4$

22. $-4 + s = 2$

23. $k - 5 = 2$

24. $-7a = -7$

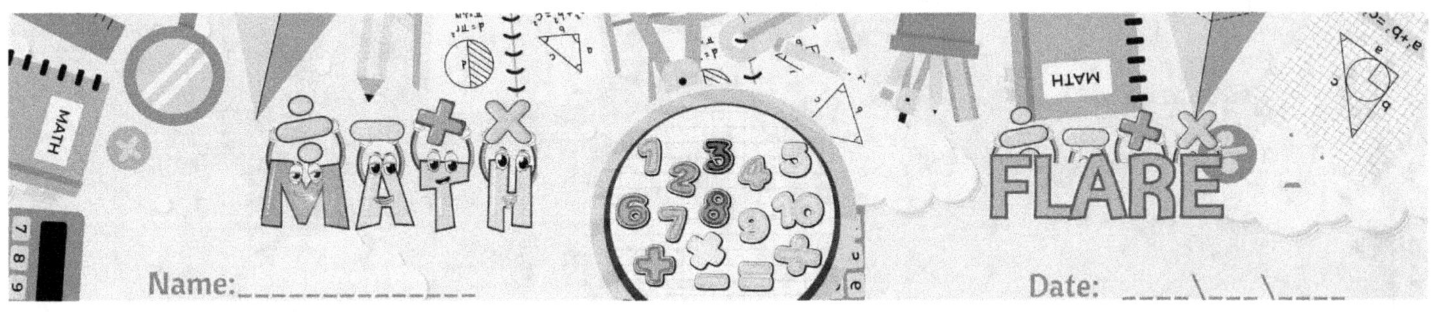

25. $z + 4 = 5$

26. $-1 = -5 + k$

27. $-70 = -10a$

28. $-5k = -20$

29. $16 = s + 9$

30. $7 = b - 3$

31. $-8b = -72$

32. $5 = -1 + s$

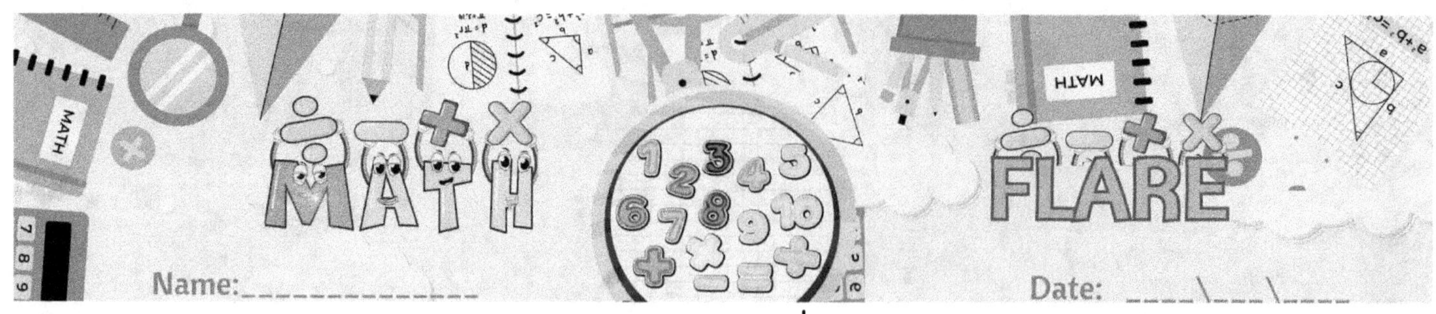

33. $-2 + b = 4$

34. $\dfrac{b}{1} = 4$

35. $a + 3 = 9$

36. $a + 9 = 11$

37. $18 = 2b$

38. $5 = \dfrac{y}{2}$

39. $y + 10 = 12$

40. $-10 = -5k$

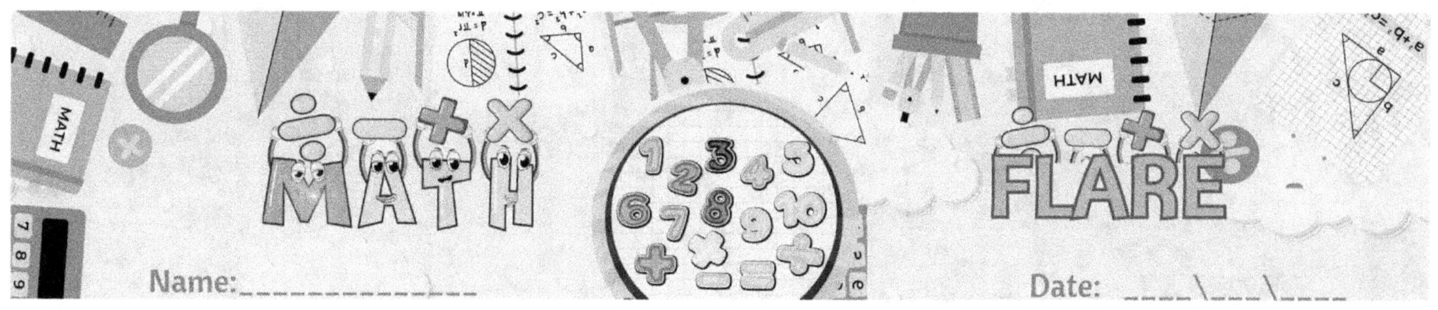

41. $3 = a - 4$

42. $-3 + a = 5$

43. $a - 6 = 2$

44. $8 = x + 1$

45. $49 = 7y$

46. $-63 = -9y$

47. $x = 6$

48. $\dfrac{z}{10} = 1$

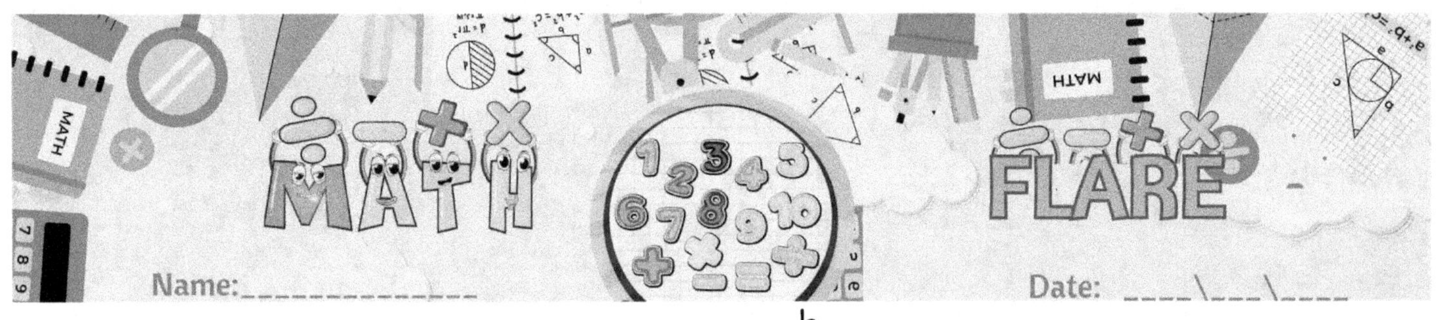

49. $36 = 4x$

50. $\dfrac{k}{1} = 1$

51. $8 = -1 + z$

52. $5 = a - 5$

53. $-1 = k - 5$

54. $-60 = -10x$

55. $-6b = -54$

56. $x - 2 = 4$

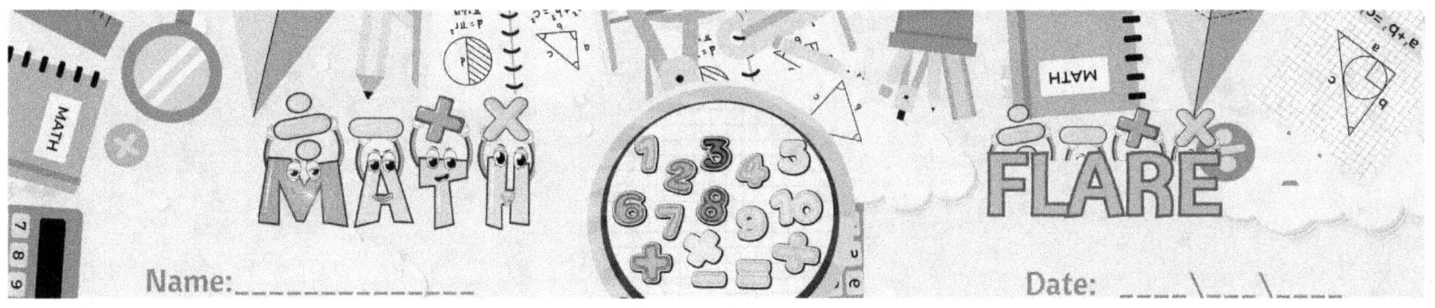

57. $-7s = -70$

58. $-8 = -10 + z$

59. $5b = 5$

60. $-6 + s = 3$

61. $-5 = k - 9$

62. $-6s = -18$

63. $\dfrac{k}{2} = 3$

64. $s - 8 = -1$

65. $\dfrac{x}{1} = 6$

66. $9 = 3b$

67. $18 = b + 8$

68. $a = 3$

69. $s + 7 = 9$

70. $b + 2 = 7$

71. $9m = 36$

72. $m + 5 = 10$

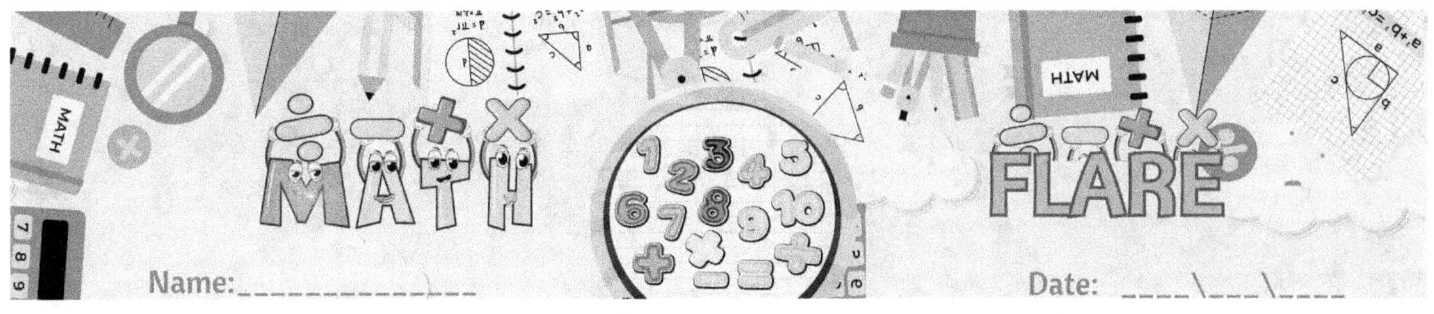

73. $19 = b + 10$

74. $-1 = k - 9$

75. $-2 + a = 1$

76. $2 = \dfrac{k}{4}$

77. $3m = 6$

78. $z + 7 = 8$

79. $3 = a - 1$

80. $\dfrac{m}{1} = 8$

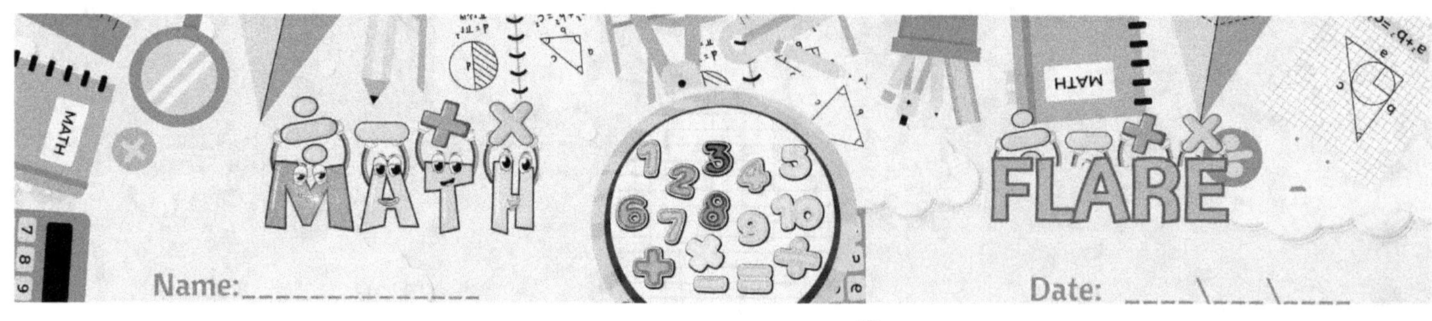

81. $7 = k - 1$

82. $1 = \dfrac{z}{8}$

83. $-2 = b - 10$

84. $-64 = -8y$

85. $2 = b - 7$

86. $28 = 4z$

87. $-9y = -81$

88. $s - 6 = -3$

89. $b = 7$

90. $-1 + a = 1$

91. $z - 2 = 8$

92. $2a = 12$

93. $-1 = -6 + z$

94. $7 = m + 1$

95. $2 = \dfrac{z}{3}$

96. $30 = 5b$

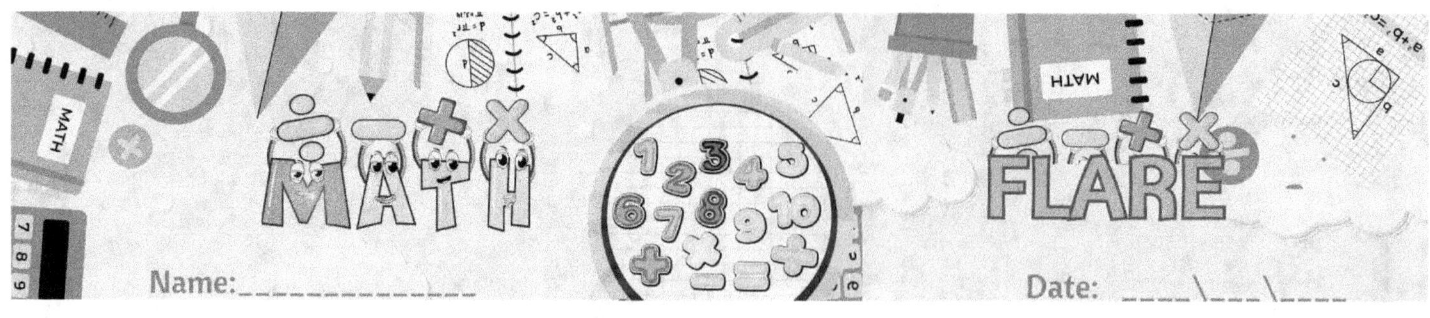

Solving Two-Step Equations

Solve for the variable.

1. $\dfrac{m}{-1} + 9 = 0$

2. $-7(-6 + a) = 35$

3. $5 = 6 - \dfrac{y}{1}$

4. $\dfrac{-6 + y}{4} = 0.5$

5. $6(1 + x) = 24$

6. $126 = (8 + a)7$

7. $-26 = -7m - 5$

8. $9 + \dfrac{y}{8} = 10$

9. $80 = -8 \dfrac{-k}{1}$

10. $4 = 1(3 + z)$

11. $-3(8 + k) = -33$

12. $\dfrac{x}{8} - 1 = 0$

13. $\dfrac{s}{1} + 8 = 9$

14. $3.6 = \dfrac{b}{-10} + 4$

15. $\dfrac{z}{1} - 4 = 4$

16. $9 = -6 \dfrac{b}{-6}$

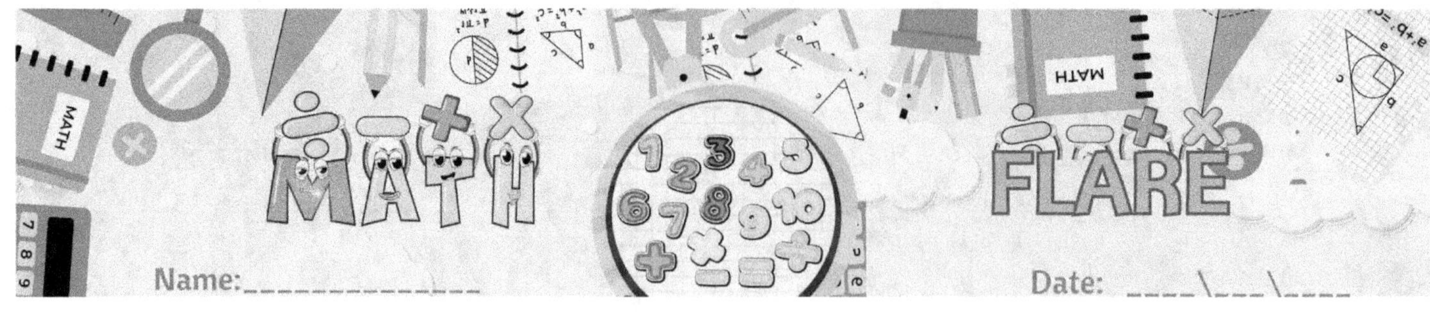

17. $62 = 9m - 1$

18. $10(-10 + m) = -70$

19. $2(7 + k) = 24$

20. $8 = \dfrac{y}{4} + 6$

21. $-9 = 9(-5 + z)$

22. $10x + 10 = 60$

23. $18 = 2(7 + z)$

24. $6\dfrac{-x}{1} = -54$

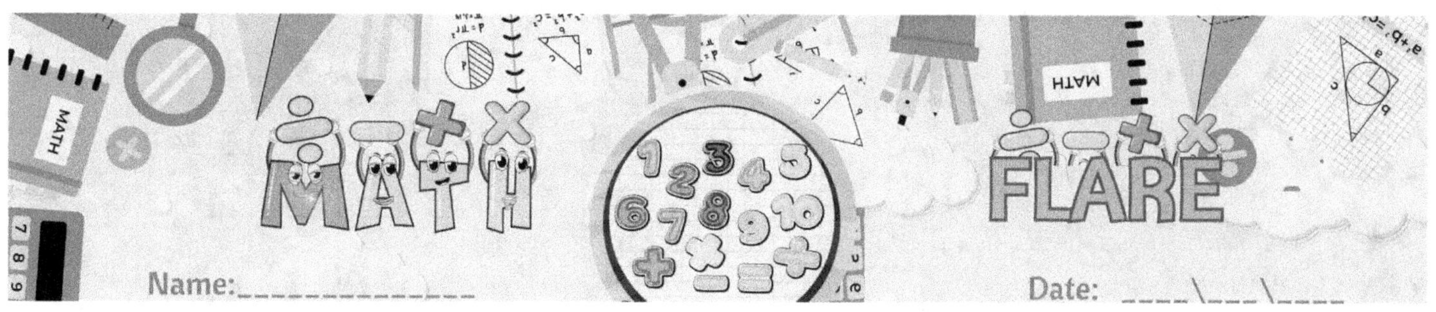

25. $10 = 1\dfrac{k}{1}$

26. $k - 4 = 6$

27. $\dfrac{-10 + x}{9} = -0.1$

28. $-x - 4 = -7$

29. $-3 = 1\dfrac{-s}{3}$

30. $(6 + y)10 = 120$

31. $-4 = (8 - m) - 2$

32. $\dfrac{10 + k}{1} = 14$

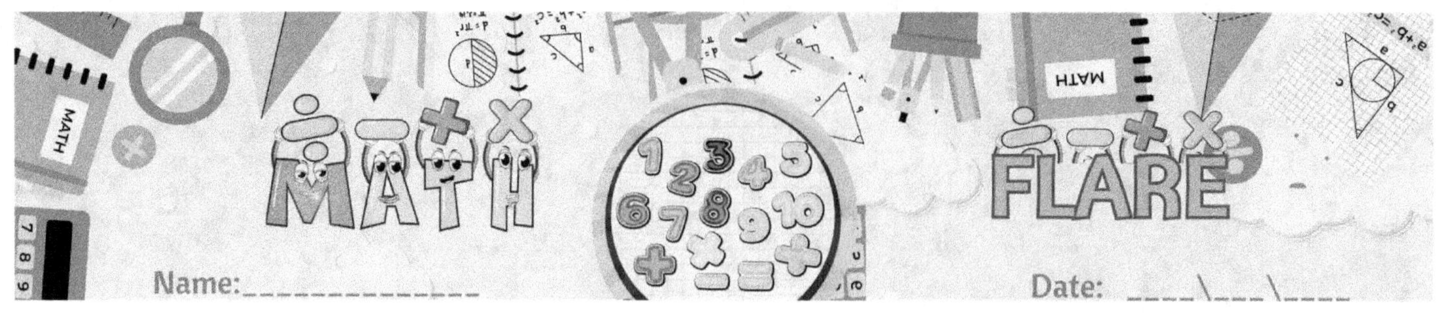

33. $-2 = 1\dfrac{-z}{4}$

34. $63 = 7(-1 + m)$

35. $55 = 6k + 1$

36. $1\dfrac{-z}{2} = -5$

37. $-8\dfrac{y}{-8} = 6$

38. $8 + \dfrac{s}{2} = 13$

39. $13 = 9 + \dfrac{s}{1}$

40. $80 = (9 + k)8$

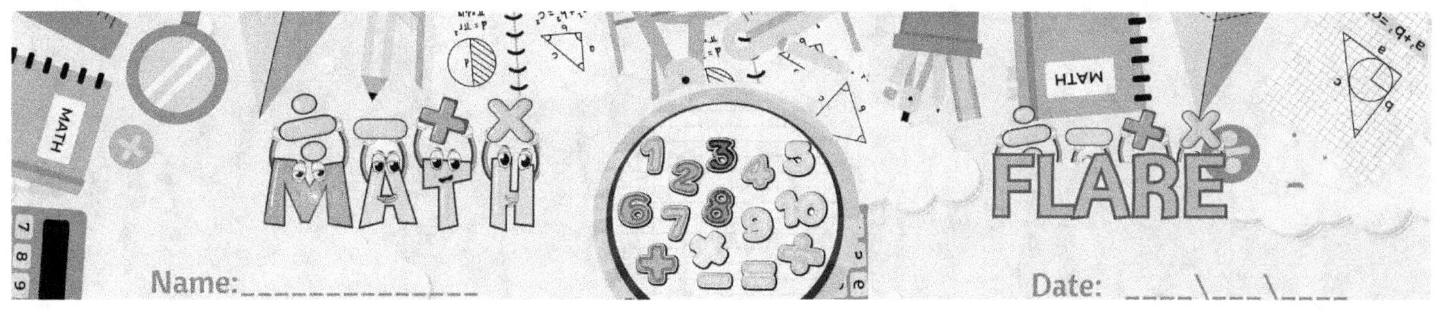

41. $35 = 7(1 + y)$

42. $2(2 - m) = -12$

43. $\dfrac{y}{-6} + 10 = 9.8$

44. $4\dfrac{-y}{4} = -8$

45. $-8(-2 + a) = 8$

46. $3s + 3 = 30$

47. $1(1 - m) = -1$

48. $3.3 = \dfrac{m}{-8} + 4$

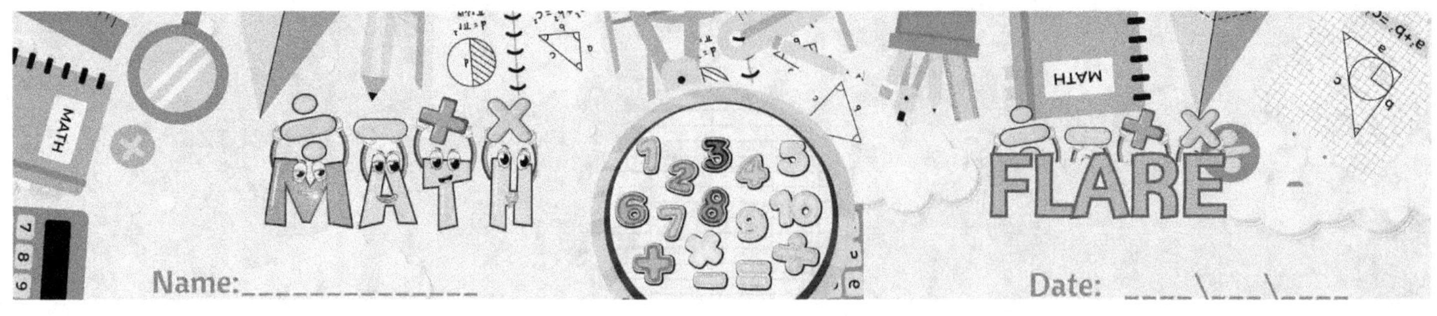

49. $-8s - 6 = -46$

50. $8\dfrac{a}{1} = 80$

51. $4(10 - b) = 28$

52. $40 = 8(9 - a)$

53. $9\dfrac{y}{8} = 9$

54. $9 = -9(-9 + k)$

55. $-6x - 8 = -44$

56. $\dfrac{x}{9} - 9 = -8$

Name:_______________

Date: _______________

57. $18 = \dfrac{x}{1} + 9$

58. $9 = \dfrac{8+s}{2}$

59. $\dfrac{m}{-4} + 4 = 1.5$

60. $42 = (1+s)7$

61. $-5x - 3 = -8$

62. $\dfrac{m}{4} - 6 = -5$

63. $-3.5 = \dfrac{6+b}{-4}$

64. $9(10 + x) = 126$

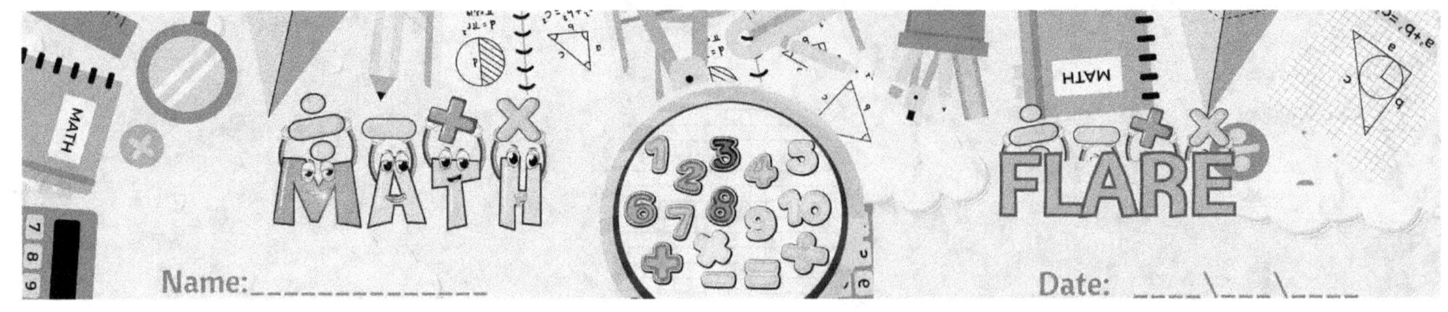

65. $27 = 9\dfrac{y}{3}$

66. $\dfrac{y}{2} - 10 = -8$

67. $17 = 9 + \dfrac{m}{1}$

68. $-6 = 6(3 - x)$

69. $9.9 = \dfrac{x}{-9} + 10$

70. $-18 = 6(-7 + k)$

71. $3(-3 + x) = 9$

72. $4 = -4\dfrac{-m}{1}$

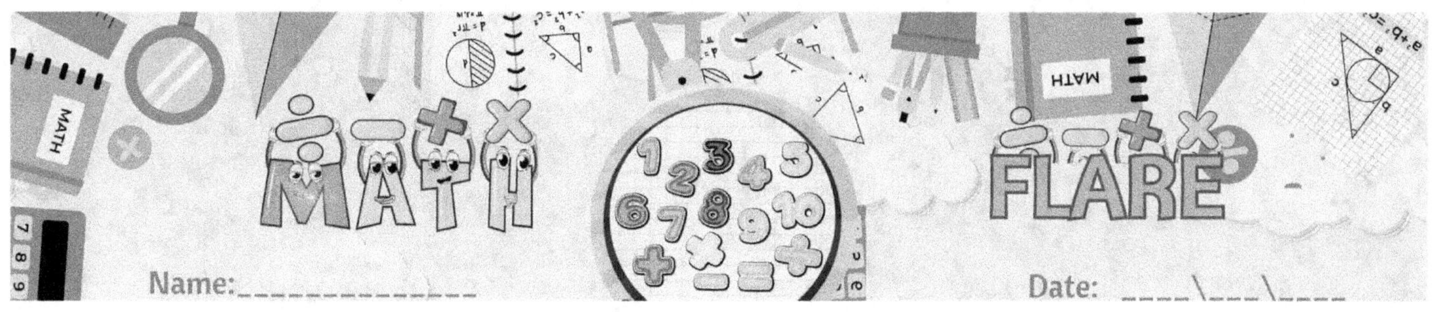

73. $7 = 6 + \dfrac{s}{1}$

74. $-4 = x - 6$

75. $24 = 4(10 - y)$

76. $(3 - m) - 4 = -10$

77. $\dfrac{8 + x}{1} = 14$

78. $-6 = 3(1 - x)$

79. $(5 + s) - 2 = 5$

80. $6\dfrac{s}{1} = 24$

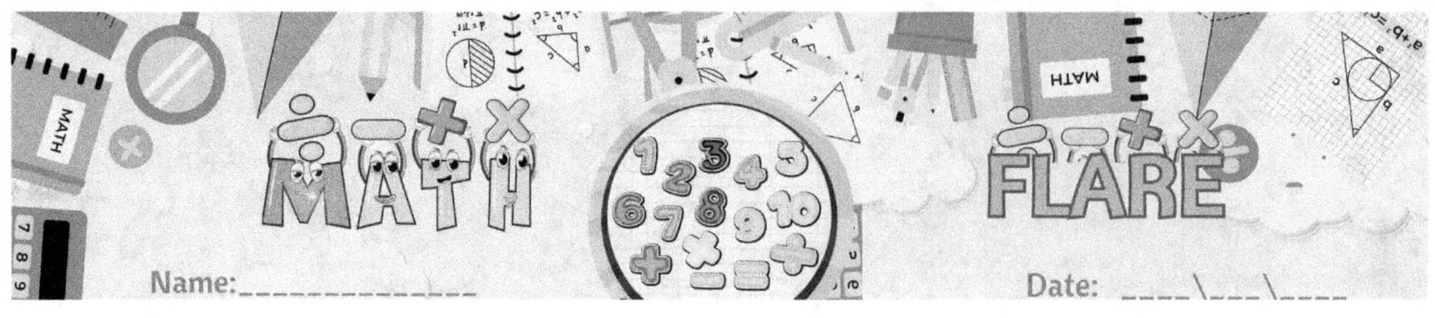

81. $34 = (8 + x)2$

82. $6\dfrac{y}{4} = 6$

83. $3s + 7 = 16$

84. $-30 = -3s - 9$

85. $-19 = -4b - 3$

86. $10 = 5(-7 + y)$

87. $-4 = 1(2 - z)$

88. $3(1 + b) = 33$

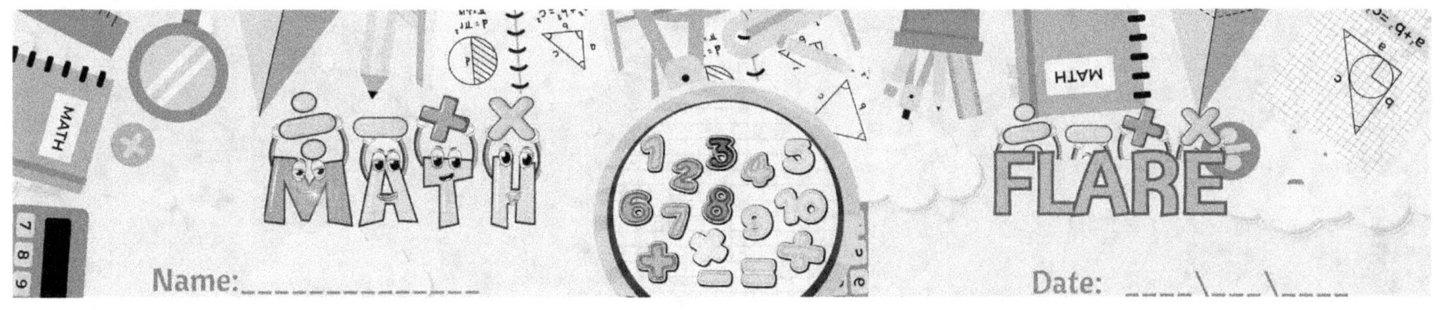

89. $-18 = -9(-1 + z)$

90. $13 = 4 + \dfrac{m}{1}$

91. $-10 \dfrac{y}{-4} = 15$

92. $-16 = 8(2 - x)$

93. $-2(10 + b) = -32$

94. $\dfrac{s}{1} - 1 = 0$

95. $8 = \dfrac{-1 + b}{1}$

96. $17 = (8 + a) - 1$

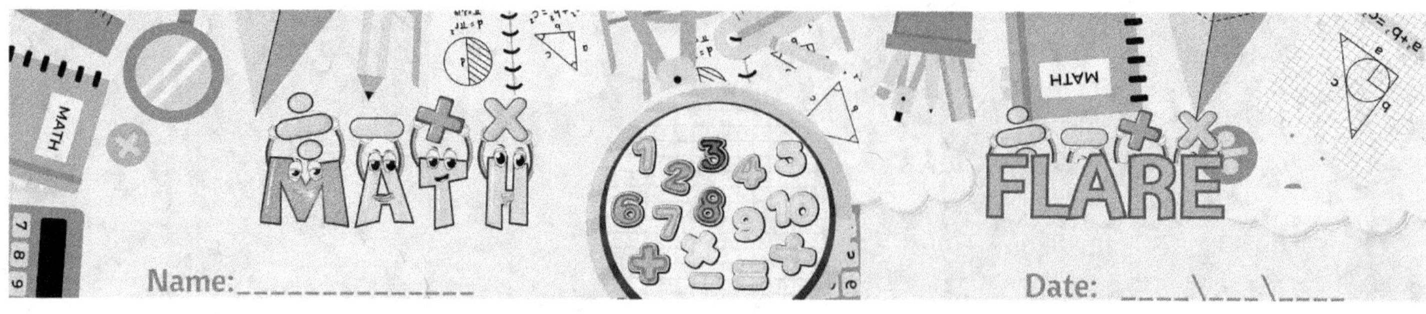

Equations: (One Side)

Solve the equations for the variable.

1. $z \div 18 = 19$

2. $-1 \times x = 3$

3. $15 - x = 13$

4. $14 - k = 12$

5. $-4 + k = 12$

6. $18 + 7y = 46$

7. $z + 14 = 33$

8. $0x - -1 = 1$

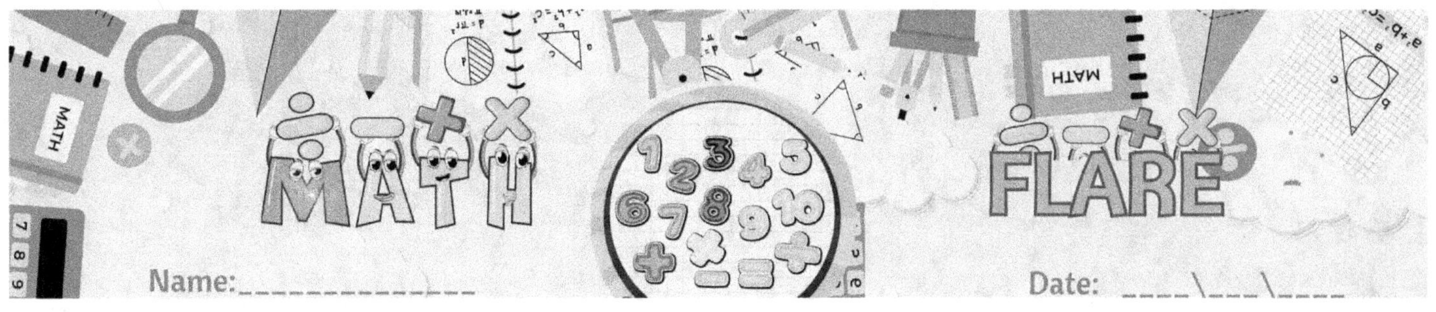

9. $-7 - -9x = 20$

10. $-3 + x = 17$

11. $k \times -4 = -40$

12. $15 - 1z = 25$

13. $15 + m = 11$

14. $y + -5 = -9$

15. $x \times 2 = 30$

16. $z \times -5 = -30$

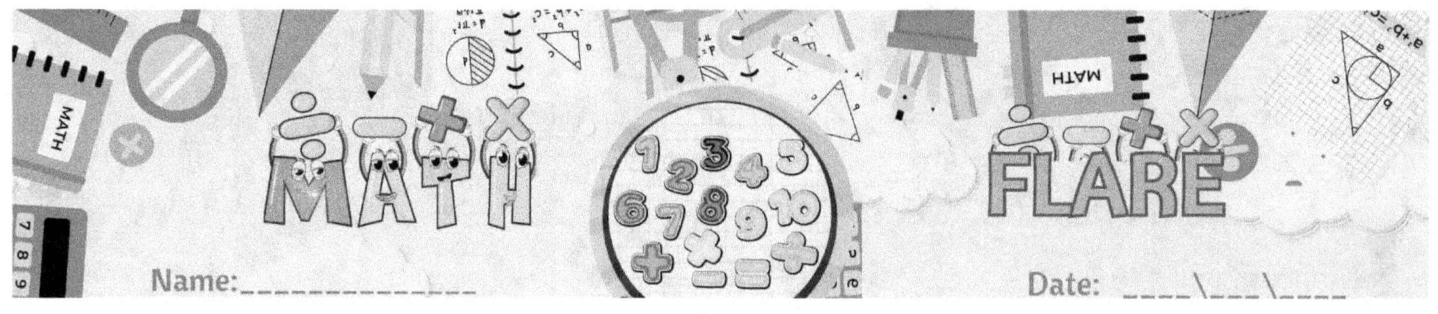

17. $y \div -6 = -8$

18. $k \times 1 = 13$

19. $m \div -5 = 4$

20. $x \div 3 = 17$

21. $8 - 18z = 188$

22. $k + 7 = 4$

23. $8 - y = 15$

24. $-2 \times y = 2$

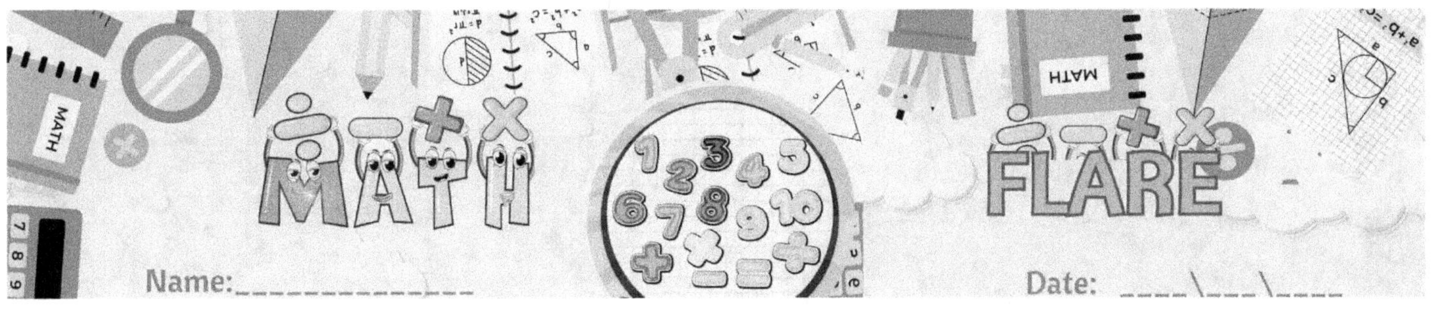

25. $6k - -10 = 94$

26. $10k - -5 = 5$

27. $3 + x = 17$

28. $98 - -10m = 8$

29. $14y + 6 = 272$

30. $48 \div k = 8$

31. $18 - y = 14$

32. $19y - -6 = 25$

33. $z - -3 = 11$

34. $7z + 0 = 49$

35. $1 + 10x = 161$

36. $2 - -10z = 182$

37. $x + 7 = -1$

38. $-48 \div z = 6$

39. $-7 \times m = -70$

40. $k \div 14 = 16$

41. $y + 15 = 34$

42. $15 \div y = 15$

43. $1 - z = 5$

44. $5y - 17 = 68$

45. $-4y + 18 = 42$

46. $4 + y = 13$

47. $y + 5 = 18$

48. $13m - 0 = 0$

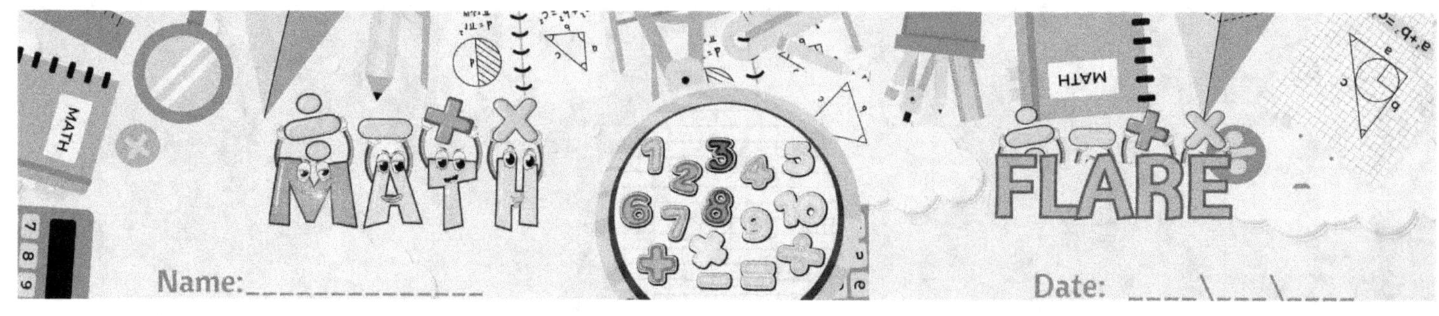

49. $18 \times x = 144$

50. $y \times 4 = 44$

51. $323 \div k = 17$

52. $-4 \div x = -2$

53. $y \div -6 = 11$

54. $9k + 10 = 154$

55. $m \div 8 = 0$

56. $y + 16 = 21$

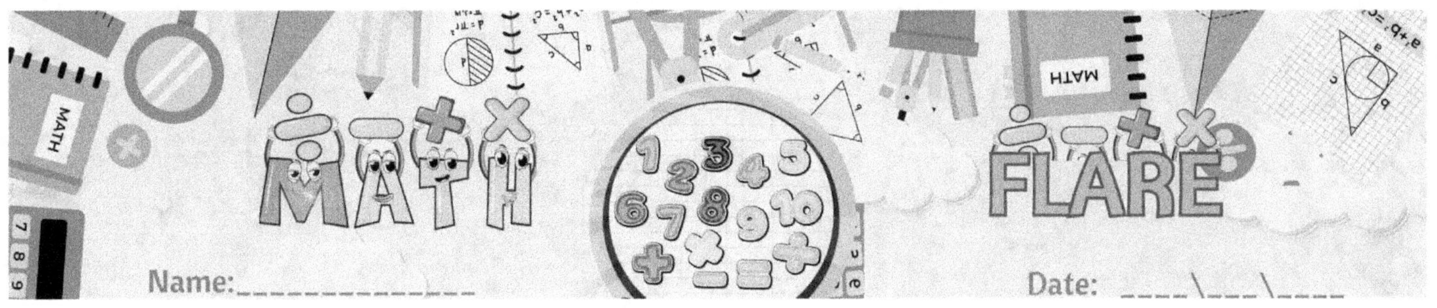

57. $z + 3 = 2$

58. $z \div 19 = -8$

59. $z \div 17 = 20$

60. $k \times 11 = -99$

61. $m \div -5 = -2$

62. $20 + 15y = -85$

63. $20 + z = 33$

64. $18 + x = 14$

65. $0 \times y = 0$

66. $4 - x = 6$

67. $k + 8 = 1$

68. $5m + 10 = -25$

69. $16m + 3 = 147$

70. $20 + -9x = -160$

71. $70 \div m = 5$

72. $9 - -6z = 99$

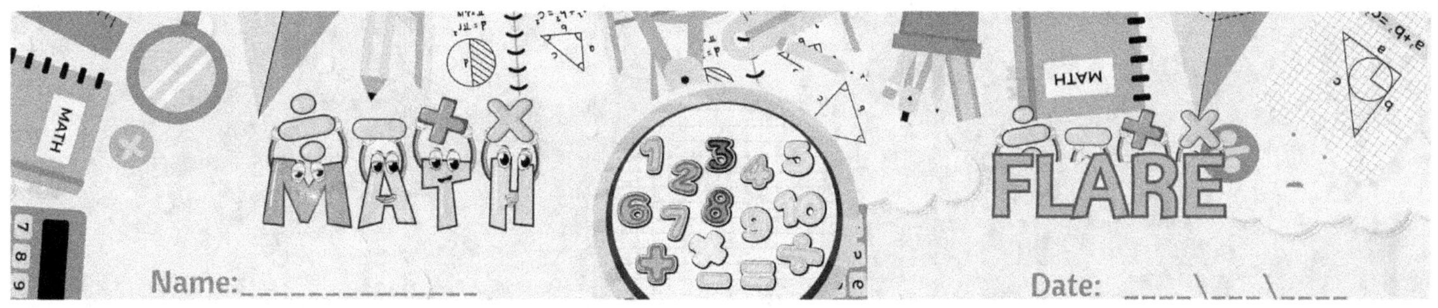

73. $205 - 11z = 7$

74. $m - -10 = 14$

75. $1 - y = 6$

76. $-1 - m = 2$

77. $m \div 2 = 15$

78. $17 \times k = 119$

79. $15z - 19 = 11$

80. $14 + -9m = 86$

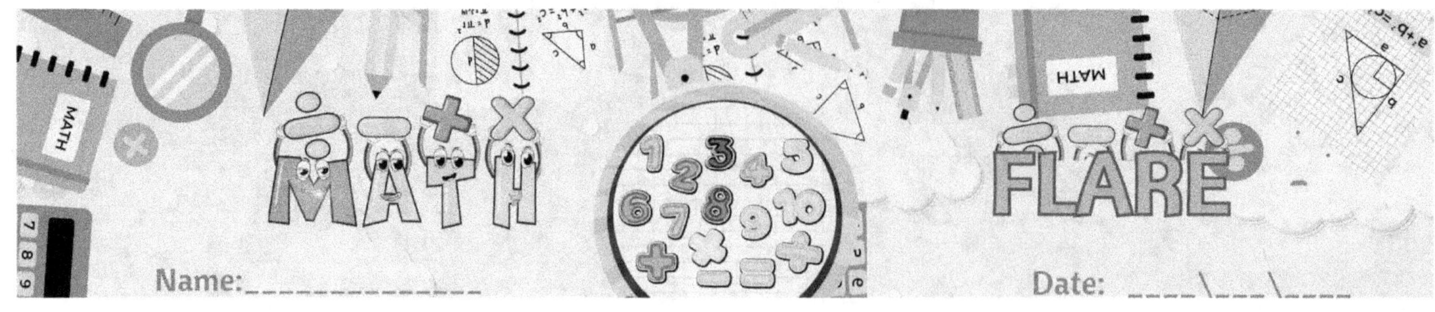

81. $19 - m = 6$

82. $6m + 18 = 138$

83. $19y + 20 = -94$

84. $k \div 1 = 4$

85. $z - -9 = 7$

86. $17m - 3 = 252$

87. $19z + 4 = -186$

88. $9 - z = 8$

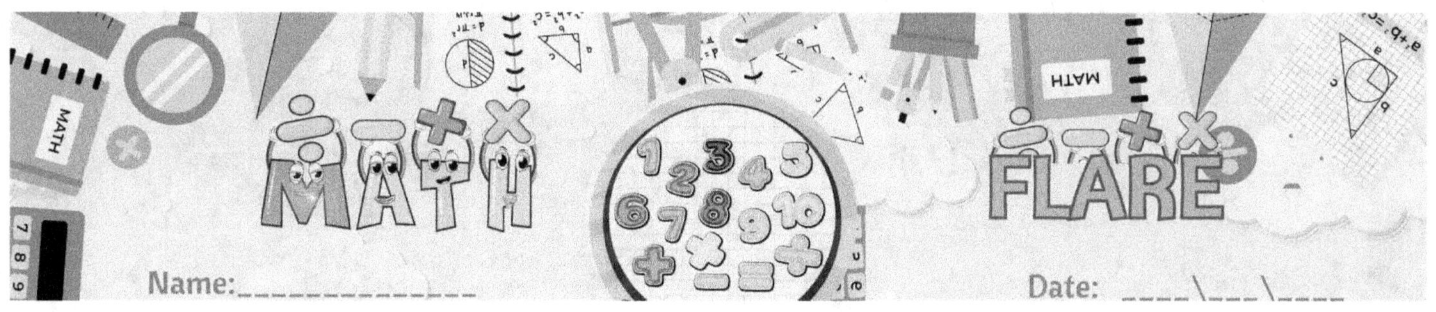

89. $-42 \div y = -6$

90. $-2 \times z = -34$

91. $3k - 9 = 0$

92. $-8 \times y = -136$

93. $4k - 12 = 0$

94. $m + 17 = 30$

95. $7 - z = 16$

96. $-9 + -5k = -59$

Evaluating Equations

Simplify the following equations when the value of n = -4

1. $\dfrac{-4 + (-48)}{n + 5} =$

2. $(n^2 + (-1)) - (-4)(-9 + n) =$

3. $-2(5 + n) =$

4. $-10n + (-1) =$

5. $3 + (-10n + 8) - 6 + (4n) =$

6. $0 + n =$

7. $1 + n =$

8. $-8(4 - n) =$

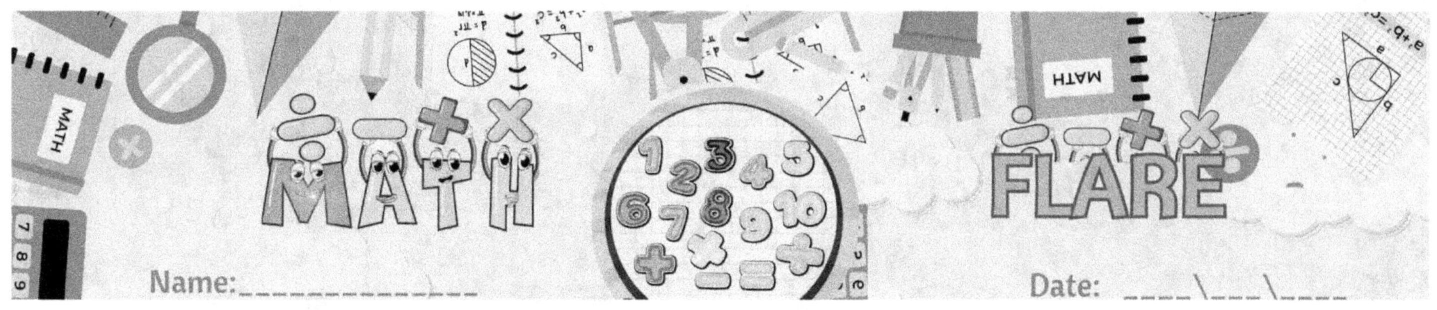

Evaluating Equations

Simplify the following equations when the value of $n = 6$

1. $-8n - n =$

2. $3(2n) =$

3. $-10 - n =$

4. $n^2 + n - (-6) =$

5. $\dfrac{n}{1} =$

6. $n + 5 + 4n =$

7. $n - (-1) =$

8. $n + 0 =$

Evaluating Equations

Simplify the following equations when the value of n = -6

1. $\dfrac{-8+n}{n+3} =$

2. $n - (-1) =$

3. $4n + 3 - 4n =$

4. $(2 + (-1)n) + (4n - 1) - (-8 + (-10)n) =$

5. $3 + 4n =$

6. $(n + (-1)) \div 3 =$

7. $\dfrac{-3+n}{n+8} =$

8. $2n + 7 =$

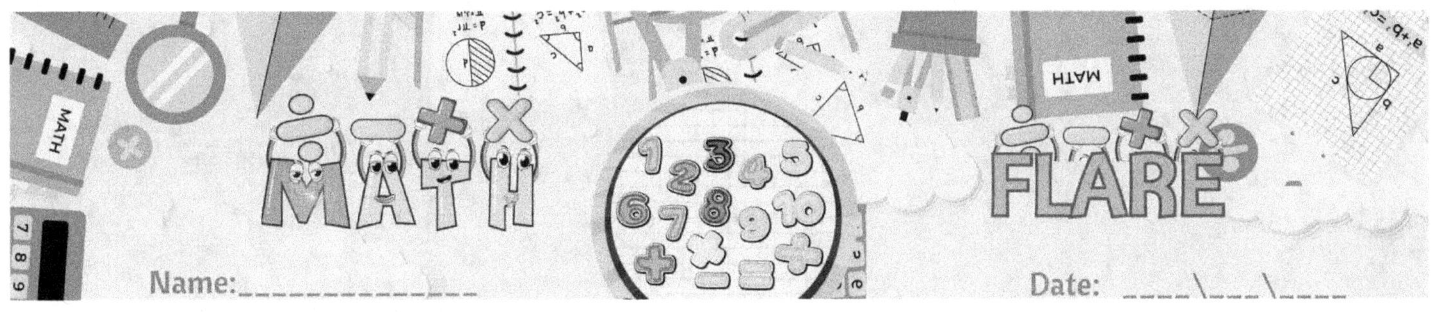

Evaluating Equations

Simplify the following equations when the value of n = -6

1. $10n + (-6)n - (-10) =$

2. $2(-2 - n) =$

3. $-5n^1 + (-4)n^3 =$

4. $3n + n =$

5. $9n - n =$

6. $(10n)^2 =$

7. $-3n + n =$

8. $2 + (-3)n =$

Name:________________   Date: ____________

Evaluating Equations

Simplify the following equations when the value of $n = -5$

1. $4n + 10 =$

2. $n - 10 =$

3. $n^1 + n - (-7) =$

4. $-9n + 0 + (-2n - 3) =$

5. $-9n + 3 =$

6. $3 + n =$

7. $-6n + 4 =$

8. $-4(-8 - n) =$

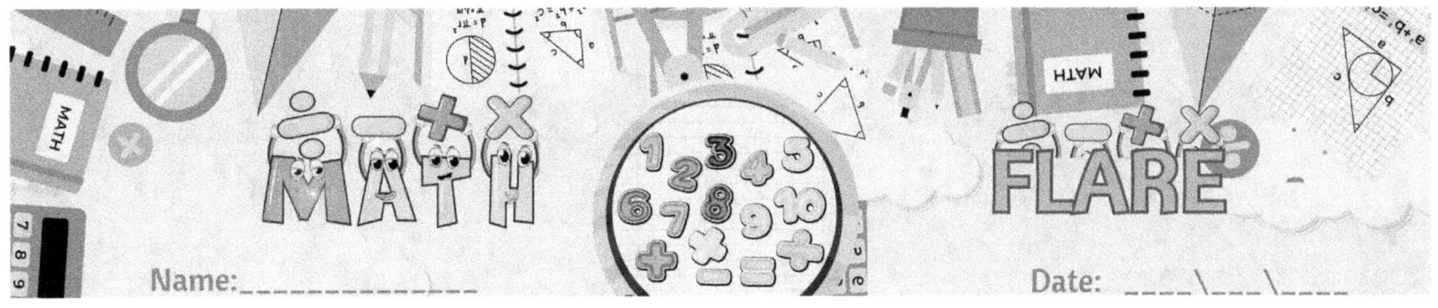

Evaluating Equations

Simplify the following equations when the value of $n = -6$

1. $5n + (-10) =$

2. $-7n + 4 =$

3. $2(2n - (-8)) + 10(1 + n) =$

4. $n^2 + n - 4 =$

5. $0(-10 + n) =$

6. $3n + (-6) =$

7. $\dfrac{n}{-6} + (-7) =$

8. $6(-6 - n) =$

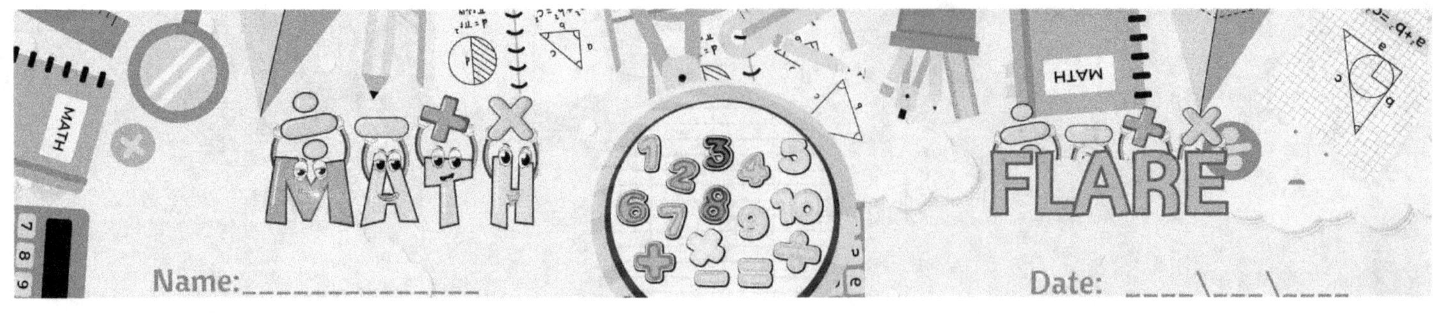

Evaluating Equations

Simplify the following equations when the value of $n = -10$

1. $(4n + (-1)) + (7n + 5) =$

2. $\dfrac{8 + n}{n + 6} =$

3. $6n + 5n + (-1)n =$

4. $-10 + n =$

5. $-4(4n - (-9)) + 0(0 + n) =$

6. $(4 + 4n) + (-10n - 6) - (-9 + 6n) =$

7. $-10(-5 - n) =$

8. $-3(5 - n) =$

Evaluating Equations

Simplify the following equations when the value of n = -1

1. $8n + 3 + (-8n - 7) =$

2. $6 + 4n =$

3. $-5^2 + n^1 =$

4. $(8n + 6) + (-7n + (-1)) =$

5. $n + 0 =$

6. $-5n + (-2) - (-6)n =$

7. $(-6n + (-2)) + (-5n - 8) =$

8. $(-7 + (-5)n) + (4n - (-7)) - (0 + 10n) =$

Evaluating Equations

Simplify the following equations when the value of n = -1

1. $2^1 + n^2 =$

2. $(8n + 1) + (8n + (-5)) =$

3. $-9n + 6n + 9n =$

4. $-5 + (-8n + 8) =$

5. $(n^1 + (-5)) - 8(3 + n) =$

6. $-4(-9n - (-6)) + (-1)(2 + n) =$

7. $(n + (-4)) \div (-5) =$

8. $-6(-1 + n) =$

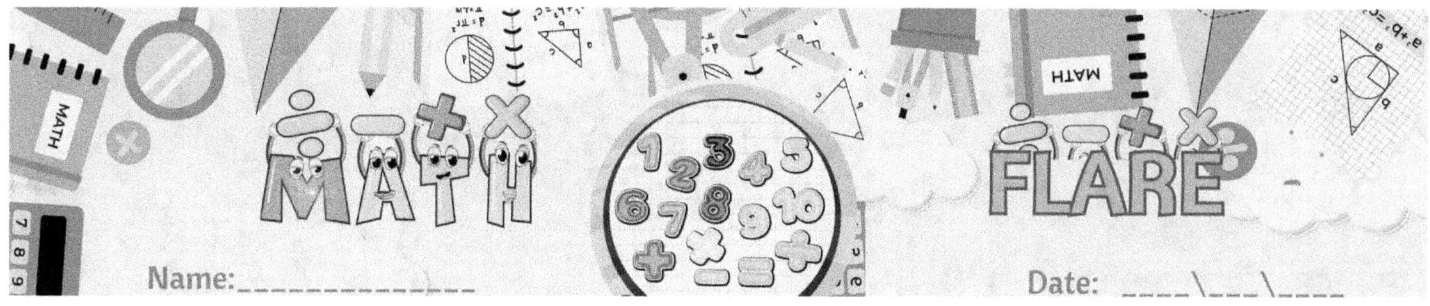

Name: _______________________   Date: _____/_____/_____

Evaluating Equations

Simplify the following equations when the value of $n = 1$

1. $-5 - n =$

2. $n \div 5 =$

3. $6n + (-4) =$

4. $4n + 1 =$

5. $n - (-10) =$

6. $6n + (-3) =$

7. $-3(-1 - n) =$

8. $-9 + \dfrac{9}{n} + 2^3 =$

ANSWERS

Page 1:   Rational Numbers: Operations

1. -19	2. 0	3. 7	4. 40	5. -1.8	6. 4	7. -23
8. 6	9. 19	10. -6	11. -0.7	12. 1	13. 0.5	14. -0.1
15. -504	16. 112	17. 48	18. 28	19. -16	20. -22	21. -4
22. -42	23. 30	24. 0.2	25. 0.7	26. -0.3	27. -14	28. 35
29. -0.8	30. 18	31. -324	32. -6	33. 16	34. 40	35. 108
36. 98	37. -13	38. -9	39. 8	40. 0	41. 8	42. -54
43. -0.3	44. -6	45. 80	46. 16	47. -18	48. 1.5	49. 21
50. -1.7	51. 0	52. -18	53. 36	54. -162	55. 12	56. 0
57. -7	58. -30					

Page 7:   Order of Operations (PEMDAS)

1. 101	2. 13	3. 144	4. 24	5. 30	6. 244
7. 13	8. 24	9. 8,101	10. 64	11. 6	12. 3,975
13. 25	14. 19	15. 15	16. 11	17. 22	18. 3,138
19. 1,605	20. 14	21. 10	22. 260	23. 59	24. 402
25. 195	26. 45	27. 187	28. 120	29. 169	30. 41
31. 1.4	32. 10	33. 5	34. 10	35. 7	36. 2,035
37. 81	38. 12	39. 144	40. 27	41. 18	42. 29
43. 140	44. 289	45. 18	46. 16	47. 85	48. 135
49. 40	50. 3	51. 130	52. 168	53. 43	54. 7

55. 33 56. 2,309 57. 6 58. 9 59. 225 60. 4

61. 1,031 62. 125 63. 3.7 64. 6 65. 0.5 66. 5,188

67. 640 68. 28 69. 10 70. 16 71. 40 72. 289

73. 104 74. 11 75. 17 76. 4 77. 0.3 78. 21

79. 36 80. 404 81. 17 82. 70 83. 108 84. 108

85. 24 86. 60 87. 3,606 88. 789 89. 2.3 90. 52

91. 92 92. 12 93. 12 94. 19 95. 19 96. 1.5

97. 425 98. 54

Page 17: Solving One-Step Equations

1. 6 2. 7 3. 2 4. 2 5. 2 6. 6 7. 6 8. 2

9. 4 10. 10 11. 9 12. 8 13. 9 14. 9 15. 10 16. 10

17. 2 18. 1 19. 5 20. 8 21. 9 22. 6 23. 7 24. 1

25. 1 26. 4 27. 7 28. 4 29. 7 30. 10 31. 9 32. 6

33. 6 34. 4 35. 6 36. 2 37. 9 38. 10 39. 2 40. 2

41. 7 42. 8 43. 8 44. 7 45. 7 46. 7 47. 6 48. 10

49. 9 50. 1 51. 9 52. 10 53. 4 54. 6 55. 9 56. 6

57. 10 58. 2 59. 1 60. 9 61. 4 62. 3 63. 6 64. 7

65. 6 66. 3 67. 10 68. 3 69. 2 70. 5 71. 4 72. 5

73. 9 74. 8 75. 3 76. 8 77. 2 78. 1 79. 4 80. 8

81. 8 82. 8 83. 8 84. 8 85. 9 86. 7 87. 9 88. 3

89. 7 90. 2 91. 10 92. 6 93. 5 94. 6 95. 6 96. 6

Page 29: Solving Two-Step Equations

1. 9	2. 1	3. 1	4. 8	5. 3	6. 10	7. 3	8. 8
9. 10	10. 1	11. 3	12. 8	13. 1	14. 4	15. 8	16. 9
17. 7	18. 3	19. 5	20. 8	21. 4	22. 5	23. 2	24. 9
25. 10	26. 10	27. 9	28. 3	29. 9	30. 6	31. 10	32. 4
33. 8	34. 10	35. 9	36. 10	37. 6	38. 10	39. 4	40. 1
41. 4	42. 8	43. 1	44. 8	45. 1	46. 9	47. 2	48. 6
49. 5	50. 10	51. 3	52. 4	53. 8	54. 8	55. 6	56. 9
57. 9	58. 10	59. 10	60. 5	61. 1	62. 4	63. 8	64. 4
65. 9	66. 4	67. 8	68. 4	69. 1	70. 4	71. 6	72. 1
73. 1	74. 2	75. 4	76. 9	77. 6	78. 3	79. 2	80. 4
81. 9	82. 4	83. 3	84. 7	85. 4	86. 9	87. 6	88. 10
89. 3	90. 9	91. 6	92. 4	93. 6	94. 1	95. 9	96. 10

Page 41: Equations: (One Side)

1. $z = 342$	2. $x = -3$	3. $x = 2$	4. $k = 2$	5. $k = 16$
6. $y = 4$	7. $z = 19$	8. $x = 8$	9. $x = 3$	10. $x = 20$
11. $k = 10$	12. $z = -10$	13. $m = -4$	14. $y = -4$	15. $x = 15$
16. $z = 6$	17. $y = 48$	18. $k = 13$	19. $m = -20$	20. $x = 51$
21. $z = -10$	22. $k = -3$	23. $y = -7$	24. $y = -1$	25. $k = 14$
26. $k = 0$	27. $x = 14$	28. $m = -9$	29. $y = 19$	30. $k = 6$
31. $y = 4$	32. $y = 1$	33. $z = 8$	34. $z = 7$	35. $x = 16$

36. z = 18   37. x = -8   38. z = -8   39. m = 10   40. k = 224

41. y = 19   42. y = 1   43. z = -4   44. y = 17   45. y = -6

46. y = 9   47. y = 13   48. m = 0   49. x = 8   50. y = 11

51. k = 19   52. x = 2   53. y = -66   54. k = 16   55. m = 0

56. y = 5   57. z = -1   58. z = -152   59. z = 340   60. k = -9

61. m = 10   62. y = -7   63. z = 13   64. x = -4   65. y = 18

66. x = -2   67. k = -7   68. m = -7   69. m = 9   70. x = 20

71. m = 14   72. z = 15   73. z = 18   74. m = 4   75. y = -5

76. m = -3   77. m = 30   78. k = 7   79. z = 2   80. m = -8

81. m = 13   82. m = 20   83. y = -6   84. k = 4   85. z = -2

86. m = 15   87. z = -10   88. z = 1   89. y = 7   90. z = 17

91. k = 3   92. y = 17   93. k = 3   94. m = 13   95. z = -9

96. k = 10

Page 53: Evaluating Equations
1. -52   2. -37   3. -2   4. 39   5. 29   6. -4   7. -3   8. -64

Page 54: Evaluating Equations
1. -54   2. 36   3. -16   4. 48   5. 6   6. 35   7. 7   8. 6

Page 55: Evaluating Equations
1. 4.7   2. -5   3. 3   4. -69   5. -21   6. -2.3   7. -4.5   8. -5

Page 56: Evaluating Equations
1. -14   2. 8   3. 894   4. -24   5. -48   6. 3,600

7. 12   8. 20

Page 57: Evaluating Equations
1. -10   2. -15   3. -3   4. 52   5. 48   6. -2   7. 34   8. 12

Page 58: Evaluating Equations
1. -40   2. 46   3. -58   4. 26   5. 0   6. -24   7. -6   8. 0

Page 59: Evaluating Equations
1. -106   2. 0.5   3. -100   4. -20   5. 124   6. 127   7. -50
8. -45

Page 60: Evaluating Equations
1. -4   2. 2   3. -26   4. 4   5. -1   6. -3   7. 1   8. 11

Page 61: Evaluating Equations
1. 3   2. -20   3. -6   4. 11   5. -22   6. -61   7. 1   8. 12

Page 62: Evaluating Equations
1. -6   2. 0.2   3. 2   4. 5   5. 11   6. 3   7. 6   8. 8